Advance Praise for *Modern Mom Probs*

"Tara is incredibly relatable, funny, and supportive. She's who I want to be when I grow up…and I'm thirty-four years old!"

—AMANDA P., Instagram's @momof1anddone

"Scrolling through Tara's account is one of the highlights of my day! She can go from making me laugh endlessly to crying happy tears because I feel less alone on this journey of motherhood."

—BECKY VIEIRA, Instagram's @wittyotter

"Tara at ModernMomProbs is a relatable, authentic, hilarious mother who brings a sigh of relief to today's mom. Visiting her page makes any mother feel like she's not alone in this wonderfully chaotic adventure of parenthood. Like a virtual hug, ModernMomProbs lifts you up in moments of mom despair, whether it be through inspirational, funny, or heartwarming posts. Tara is a true delight; one I may not have met if it weren't for this amazing community she's built, and I'm so lucky I can call her a friend. Quite simply, the powerful message Tara brilliantly conveys through ModernMomProbs is, 'You got this, Mama.'"

—DEB BIONDOLILLO, Instagram's @stamfordmommy

MODERN
Mom Probs

A SURVIVAL GUIDE
FOR 21ST CENTURY MOTHERS

TARA CLARK

Post Hill
PRESS

A POST HILL PRESS BOOK
ISBN: 978-1-64293-758-9
ISBN (eBook): 978-1-64293-759-6

Modern Mom Probs:
A Survival Guide for 21st Century Mothers
© 2021 by Tara Clark
All Rights Reserved

Illustrations by Mary McConville

Post Hill Press
New York • Nashville
posthillpress.com

Published in the United States of America
1 2 3 4 5 6 7 8 9 10

This book is dedicated to modern moms
everywhere who inspire me every day.

Table of Contents

Chapter 2. Sleep Probs

Chapter 3. Meal Probs

Chapter 4. Kid Probs

Chapter 5. You Probs

Chapter 6. Friend Probs

Chapter 7. Relationship Probs

Chapter 8. Tech Probs

Chapter 9. Travel Probs

Chapter 10. I Got 99 Problems, But Motherhood Ain't One...207

Foreword

I'm sure you have heard the common phrase: children don't come with instructions. Well, thanks to Tara Clark, now they do. And not just baby instructions—I'm talking kids, meals, vacations, your pelvic floor, too much screen time, bully problems (for you and your kid), and even intimacy. The pages of this book will get you through the things you expect to be thrown your way and many that you've never even dreamed of.

I met Tara Clark when researching mom groups for my latest novel, *Eliza Starts a Rumor*. Eliza is the moderator of a fictional mom group just as Tara is the moderator of Modern Mom Probs, so the synchronicity was obvious. I was immediately taken by her energy and straightforward approach. Tara's wit, humor, and common-sense style will have you laughing instead of crying and moving forward knowing that you are not alone and that a zillion other moms have been down the same road as you.

Modern Mom Probs supplies a bevy of pertinent information in a way that keeps you interested as if you were reading a juicy novel or scrolling through the posts on your local online moms' group. And her detailed table of contents makes it easy to find just what you are looking for. This is not your mother's parenting book, which is good because your mother didn't have to deal with half of what you do. Let's face it, with all of the things thrown at parents today, the old playbooks should be tossed aside. If you are looking for a new one, you are in the right place.

Jane L. Rosen
Author of *Nine Women, One Dress* and
Eliza Starts a Rumor

Preface

Welcome! Hello there!

When I conceived of this book, I never imagined that I would have written the bulk of it during a global pandemic and racial justice movement. As I drafted chapter after chapter, I asked myself whether I should scrap the whole project completely because of a reality where school pickups and meandering Target aisles were no longer immediate concerns of mine or yours. Would this book be tone deaf? Would it depress me to write it as a longing for days gone by? Would it upset people to read it? Would it anger them? I worried that the worst thing I could do at a time like this was produce this book.

But then it occurred to me that one day, life *would* get back to normal, and maybe even a better normal. Being a parent is the ultimate exercise in optimism. We are optimistic that our seven-pound baby girl will become president someday. We are optimistic that our seven-year-old spirited son will use that spirit to change the world. So I remain optimistic that being part of a motherhood community and sharing a laugh together may be exactly what we need during these complicated times.

In what follows, I've chosen 99 problems facing modern mothers. Some of these chapters are intended to be a pure laugh where I share my take on important topics, such as which fast food joint makes the best chicken nuggets (based on intensive, totally subjective research). In other chapters, we get serious and tackle real concerns of mothers, like postpartum depression, sleep troubles, and screen time. Where possible, I have interviewed experts on topics that I believed deserved professional treatment. And where unnecessary, it's all me, baby!

You can skip around to the chapters that speak to you, or if you want to, you can read them in order. (I won't judge.) These chapters are meant to be short and sweet, enjoyed during naptime or sitting in the car awaiting school pickup (is that a thing again yet?). However you decide to tackle this book, I hope you enjoy it and that you laugh, cry, and maybe learn a thing or two, because motherhood is like that.

Introduction

And now, a word from your tour guide...

I'm Tara, your tour guide on the wild adventure of modern mom problems. Yes, these tend to be "first-world problems" and are meant to make you smile and think, not solve all of the world's challenges in one sitting.

We, as twenty-first century mothers, face a myriad of both hilarious and serious problems that our mothers and grandmothers never faced and some that they did, all while doing it without much of an in-person village. Our village has moved online. That's where @modernmomprobs comes in. In the Instagram community each day, I come in contact with thousands of mothers sharing their motherhood experiences. The good, bad, and oh, damn, did that really happen?! Social media is a living laboratory of thoughts, creativity, and public opinions. It is where we now gather as our modern moon lodge.

But women have always gathered. Whether in sewing circles or around the kitchen table, moms have discussed motherhood, childbirth, sexuality, and all the things significant in their lives. We share our fears, joys, and hopes. So it's clear that what we do at @modernmomprobs is not a new concept, only a new space. As modern mothers, it's often hard to find solutions to problems our kids face with things we have no background for understanding (have you ever seen common core math before?). We don't have the same family structure or same neighborhood structure as previous generations, and the world is just getting more and more complicated due to new technologies and increased expectations.

Modern motherhood is hard. *Period.* Many modern moms can admit, "I love my kids more than anything. I just don't love every second of being a mom."

Babies don't come with an official instruction manual like a Chrysler Pacifica. A hard-fast manual that states, "If this happens, do that," and it will work 100 percent of the time. People don't work like that. Sure, you may have a pile of books to thumb through, but never *actually* read cover to cover, and there's the internet, which is full of people arguing about everything that will make you anxious and more confused than when you started your original search. So you may as well do what you think is best for your children. Do the things that feel right to do, and most importantly, surround yourself with people who make you laugh and realize things really are going to be ok.

Our online mom community has done that for me and countless others. This book is an extension of that online community and will be readable even in that one dead spot where you can't get Wi-Fi. You know the one I am talking about. The one that takes the kids a little bit longer to find you hiding in?

We're going to tackle 99 problems, like the Jay-Z song, "99 Problems." And by the end I think we will all agree, we got 99 problems but motherhood ain't one! We got this, mamas!

What Is a Modern Mom Prob?

Modern Mom Prob: (noun) an unwelcome, uncomfortable, or inconvenient situation or problem experienced by a parent in the twenty-first century. The problems are generally, but not always, characterized by technology, social media, big box stores, overpriced coffee, or nonsensical internal pressures that nineteenth century moms would scoff at.

DIAGRAM OF A MODERN MOM*

MESSY HAIR BUN

A FEW GRAY HAIRS

DARK UNDER-EYE CIRCLES

OVERPRICED
CAFFEINATED
BEVERAGE

OFFSPRING
IN CARRIER

BABY SPIT-UP
ON SOFT
COTTON SHIRT

BLACK
LEGGINGS
FOR
COMFORT
AND STAIN
COVERAGE

SHOPPING BAG FROM
BIG-BOX STORE

COMFORTABLE FOOTWEAR
FOR CHASING KIDS AND
WALKING BABY TO SLEEP

*This representation in no way depicts all modern moms.
For illustration purposes only.

WARNING!

This survival guide is not a scientific treatise on mothering, child-birth, breastfeeding, child development, universal laws of physics, nor is it the key to parenting, uncovered from an ancient Egyptian tomb. This book is absolutely not to be construed as containing real medical advice. The only doctorate I have is in legging design and upkeep (honorary degree). If you're looking for medical advice, consult your local Facebook Moms' group*. They will diagnose everything from rashes to scalp lacerations, regardless of medical training.

---

* Consulting your local Facebook Moms' Group is *not* actually advised for true medical advice. JUST SO WE ARE CLEAR.

This survival guide is now in your possession. Keep it safe from:

* Infant slobber

* Spit-up breast milk

* Hungry dogs

* Scented rainbow markers

* Rogue Sharpies

* Chewed-up Cheetos

This book is not intended for:

A. Sanctimommies*

B. Zombies (though mombies** are welcome)

C. Eighteenth Century Mothers

D. Unicorns (though unicorn moms*** are welcome)

Now let's dive in!

---

* Sanctimommies are highly opinionated mothers who are quick to let you know the "right way" of raising your children via their unsolicited advice. They are going to be very unhappy with this book as they are with most things related to parenting, unless they wrote it.

** A mombie is a sleep-deprived mom who moves so slowly, she resembles a zombie. She may be identified by a caffeinated beverage in hand, disheveled clothing, and a mom bun. She may need help knowing where she is from time to time but will not attack.

*** A unicorn mom is "a mother who's not perfect, enjoys alcohol, has a sense of humor, and couldn't care less what you think. See also: Beautiful; Boss; Bitch & Zero F#&ks Given" (courtesy of Maria Hunt from @UnicornMoms). This mom is a heavy reader of the chapters to follow and could add ninety-nine more.

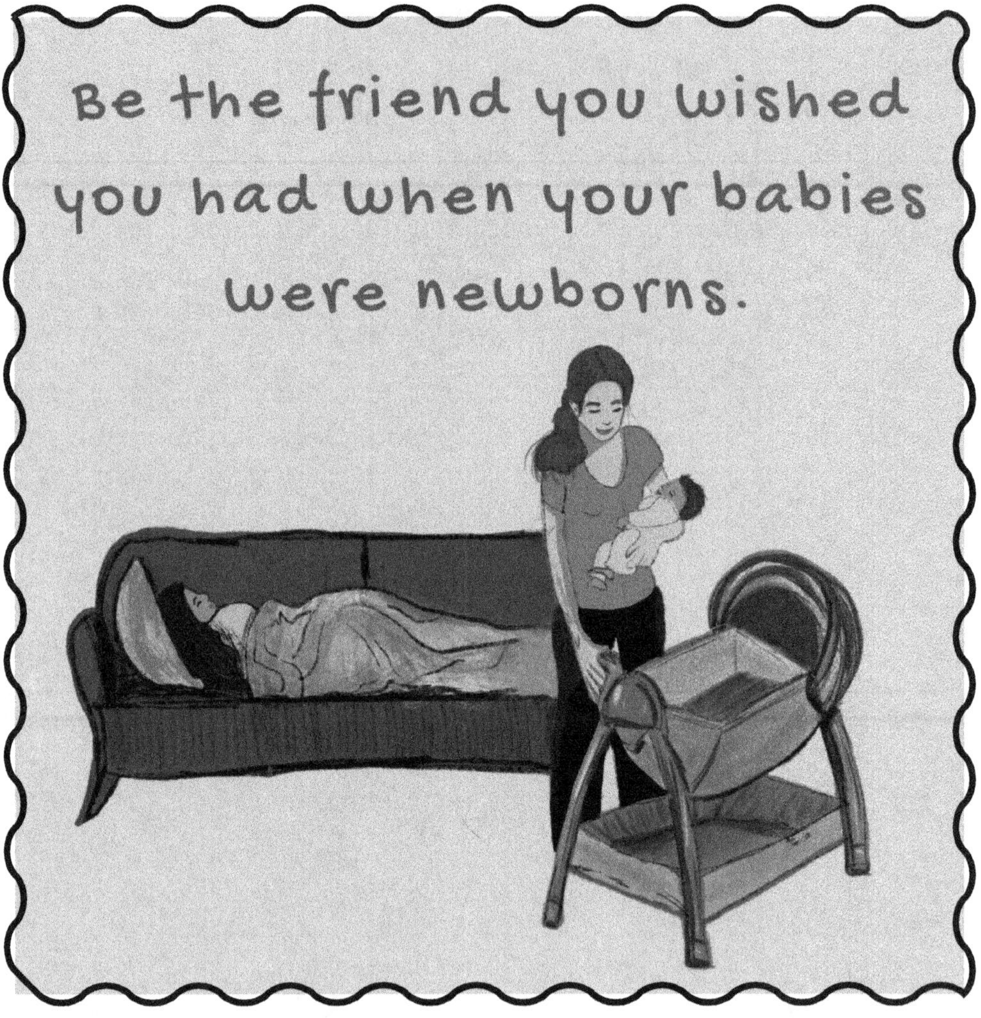
Be the friend you wished
you had when your babies
were newborns.

Chapter 1

BABY PROBS

*T*his chapter centers around your new bundle of poop-making, chubby-cheek-having, wake-you-up-every-two-hours-until-your-brain-hurts bundle of joy. Read these chapters multiple times; sleep deprivation has been shown to jack up your memory. What? Did I already say the memory part?

#1. GREAT EXPECTATIONS

"You're expecting? How nice!"

"So, are you expecting little Lucy to go to medical school like Dad?"

Isn't it funny that we say we're "expecting" when we're pregnant? What are we expecting to happen, besides a baby being born? And what are we expecting out of this yet-to-be-born person, exactly? And what is expected of us, as new mothers?

Well, don't worry. The internet will tell you exactly what to expect. As will family and friends, and maybe even some random stranger behind you in the grocery store checkout line. As will your own non-stop internal monologue. And so begins the long and harrowing journey of the mother.

Expectations on you. Expectations on your kids. And very little answer as to what to do when you fall short of those expectations. In fact, a misalignment of expectations and reality is at the core of most of what our modern mom problems are…but more about that in the subsequent chapters.

When my husband and I were engaged, we were required to do some pre-marriage classes at our local church. At first we thought, why do we have to do this? For one class, we met with a lovely older couple, and I have to say, their advice has gotten us through all manner of challenges, including parenthood. They told us, in no uncertain terms, *lower your expectations*. Of each other. Of your future. Of your concept of wedded bliss. Of what your kids will or will not be and do. Of how they will behave. Of whether or not they will even be your biological children. Just love each other and appreciate one another, no strings attached.

In Ron Fournier's book *Love That Boy: What Two Presidents, Eight Road Trips, and My Son Taught Me About a Parent's Expectations*, he describes his journey as the father of a child on the autism spectrum. He tackles the tremendous level of expectations we put on ourselves and our kids in the modern "sport" of parenting. All of the expectation-mongering we face prevents us from getting down to the real business of parenting, in his particular case, that he only needed to "love that boy."

That baby in your belly may not actually be the person you had in mind. That newborn in your stroller may not behave how you imagined. They may (probably, *will*) struggle. I'm going to repeat that: they will struggle. In some way, shape, or form they will prove that being an individual means you are not perfect, or even typical, in all ways.

Your child will fall short of some of your expectations, that is a certainty. That you will fall short of your own expectations as a mother is also quite certain. But how, you may wonder, do I deal with that?

I'll tell you what has worked for me. Lower your expectations. Love yourself. And love that child.

EXPECTATIONS SCALE

#2. Gender Reveal Parties, Ripped from the Headlines

When I think back to 2008, I think about the major crisis that gripped the world at that time. The subprime mortgage-induced financial crisis?? No. I'm referring to the very first documented gender reveal party, thrown by blogger Jenna Karvunidis. The story goes, thebump. com shared her idea, and the rest is blue and pink history.

If you have been living under a rock or haven't looked at social media in the last decade, here is a little reminder. A gender reveal party is when you invite everybody over and dramatically reveal if you're having a boy or a girl. Ok, great, now we're all on the same page. I have to say, gender reveal parties can be cute. But like anything, there's always a subset of people that ruin, well, everything.

If you have a great gender reveal party planned or did some dramatic reveal, I'm not trying to be a hater, but I am trying to implore you: don't set over forty-five thousand acres of land on fire! Seriously.

Here are some real headlines about gender reveal parties gone wrong. I hope you will make the right decision after reading these and having a laugh:

"Elderly woman told her son she was going to a 'sex party', turns out the truth was a lot less exciting"

Oof. To be a fly on the wall for that conversation. No grandma, it's called a gender reveal party; you can put the fishnets back in the drawer. Yikes.

"Arizona Border Patrol Agent Accidentally Starts Wildfire"

Believe it or not, shooting a target designed to release blue or pink powder, in the middle of a scorching hot desert, may inadvertently lead to a wildfire that damages forty-seven thousand acres of land and causes $8 million in damages. All so Aunty Liz can get a picture of your plume of pink smoke? Nah.

"A Family Gets Up Close and Personal with An Alligator's Jaws"

You gave a live gator a watermelon full of blue or pink Jell-O? That seems…aggressive.

"'Use a bit of common sense': A gender-reveal party stunt ends with a car erupting in flames"

Well, I guess a car explosion isn't as bad as forty-seven acres of land? How did that happen?!?

"Pregnant Mom Smacked in Face with Baseball Bat in Gender Reveal Gone Wrong" Congratulations on the baby girl!!! You want a frozen steak for that shiner, or what?

"Air Cannon Injures Dad-to-Be's Groin"

Better make this pending baby your last, bruh. Nothin's doin' down there after that blue crotch-rocket comes to town.

"Woman hit with dart during gender reveal gone wrong"

The story goes: dart passes through a balloon full of colored confetti, confetti flies out (yay!), dart continues into the foot of a party-goer. Seems entirely predictable and also, wholly unnecessary.

And finally, this simple headline, from *The Atlantic*.

"How Many People Have to Die Before We're Done With Gender Reveals?"

Talk about questions you never thought we'd need to ask ourselves.

I rest my case. If you must, go ahead and buy a pink or blue cake. But don't crash your crop duster into a cornfield just to do a gender reveal (yeah, that happened once, too).

Sunday, August 30, 2020

Gender Reveal Party Fiasco

Hate to say, "I told you so," but I totally did!   Rei
foll

#3. Picking the Right Baby Name

Yeesh. What am I gonna call this thing? The menagerie of personal, religious, and cultural origins of choosing a name is truly impressive and bewildering. You're going to put a name on the birth certificate at some point, so it's all very official. And without fail, you will tell someone your child's name, and they will have some story about a great aunt's first husband's neighbor who had that name and was horrible. Sadly, I can't really help you pick the "right" name for your bundle of joy (maybe an online name generator or a character from your favorite show?). But I can help you out with the other name(s) your kid will acquire: the cutesy little nicknames we all end up having for our little ones. Personally, we call our little guy quackle be-dackle, but no judgment if you go another way on this.

Chart 1: Use the first letter of your first name to determine your baby's first name.

A	Wrinkles
B	Dimples
C	Happy
D	Squirt
E	Smiley
F	Poops
G	Toes
H	Tush

Chart 2: Use the first letter of your last name to determine your baby's middle name.

A	Milklover
B	Diaperbaby
C	Bumbum
D	Poopsiedoo
E	Sweet toes
F	Blowout
G	Numnums
H	Snotty

I	Crawly	I	Chunkylegs
J	Small Fry	J	Tubstubs
K	Cuddles	K	Boogerbottom
L	Cryer	L	Hairbowbooboo
M	Huggies	M	Dinkydoodoo
N	Tooty	N	Wiggles
O	Snuggles	O	Snuggy
P	Gums	P	Swaddlewrap
Q	Cheeks	Q	Laughsnort
R	Nappy	R	Fannysprinkles
S	Boomboom	S	Bubblecheeks
T	Stinker	T	Milkbreath
U	Skippy	U	Diaperbutt
V	Giggles	V	VonCutey
W	Kissies	W	Wrinkleface
X	Binky	X	Cutiepie
Y	Nummy	Y	Ticklesfart
Z	Wuggy	Z	Bubblywubbly

Congratulations on your new baby, Wrinkles McWrinkleface!

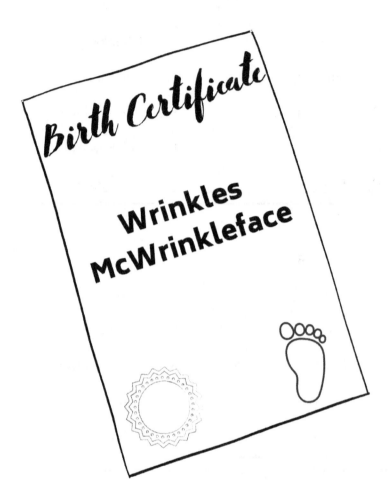

#4. Gettin' That Baby Out

For the purposes of this chapter, let's make the assumption that you are pregnant, were pregnant, or could be pregnant sometime in the future. Let's also assume that you read about pregnancy health tips, sleep techniques, and "how to rock that pregnancy glow."

Well, that's a different book altogether. If you want some real sh*t about getting the baby out of your body because she's overstayed her welcome in the womb, then step right up!

There's a lot of pressure to be the natural holistic prego goddess wearing a flower crown in the forest, birthing that perfect cherub while woodland creatures sing harmoniously and gather 'round. The truth is that the most important thing is delivering a healthy baby, by any means necessary. And ideally, *you* should also survive childbirth. It's only fair!

Why do we feel this pressure to be like a goddess giving birth? Social media, mainstream media, and family/societal pressures. End of story. "They" have decided that birthing a baby isn't a natural and completely arduous biological process, but a photo op for you to document somewhere (and rarely look at again). You know all of this is bullsh*t, right? So, step one is to ignore this stuff from the outset and stop it from leading you down a garden path that risks you and the baby's health or adds undue pressure to an already very stressful life event. Pinterest did *not* invent childbirth. Period. And Pinterest will not be there to help you push, push, push.

We all love plans, we're modern moms (or moms-to-be). Let's now consider Birth Plans. I have two friends who had elaborate birth plans (one for a home birth, the other for a local hospital). As their respective labors progressed, many unexpected things happened. Suddenly, both babies' and mothers' lives were at risk as they clung to their plans. One friend nearly died at home and required intensive care in the hospital, and the other's baby was delivered using the rarely-deployed method of forceps birth.

Luckily, everybody is ok today. But the point is, plans change. Their birth plans were very focused on the best-case-scenario, but they had to pivot when things changed. You may not end up in a best-case-scenario. Make some plans for nice music and scents that you like. Get some candles and oils. Whatever you like. But please be safe and remember while we may have delivered babies for thousands of years without doctors' help, many of us would not be alive today without that same help.

Last but not least, let's consider epidurals and C-sections. Years and years of research and hundreds of scientific manuscripts later, we're pretty darn sure these are safe procedures for you and for your baby. Horror stories exist, but for every horror story there are literally thousands of mundane non-stories about a comfortable/tolerable childbirth via the wonders of anesthesia. You can admit you don't want to push until you're blue from the pain and request an epidural. You can also admit that maybe having a C-section is not an "easy way out" and is perhaps the safest thing for you and the baby. Do what you feel most comfortable with, and not what your mother-in-law thinks is the "right" way to labor (or what stipulation 21-b says in your birth plan).

My bottom-line advice to you is plan for the birth of your dreams full of candles, soothing music, and woodland creatures. BUT please be prepared to deviate from the plan if you or your baby's life is at risk. Have a solid plan B and maybe even a plan C.

REMEMBER OUR NUMBER ONE GOAL: GET THE BABY OUT SAFELY AND KEEP MOM SAFE, TOO. Five years after all your plans went to sh*t and you're playing with your beautiful child, you won't look at their face and think, "I can't believe I forgot that lavender candle."

#5. The All-Important, Oft-Disappointing Newborn Pictures

So, you got the baby out. Congratulations! Now you're supposed to start documenting it! Did a birth really even happen if it wasn't documented by a thousand photos neatly archived in a Dropbox folder?

My son is, to me, a thing of beauty. But those newborn photos are really, pretty, well, uh, they're something. Trade secret: the actual purpose of newborn pictures is to have a record of the shriveled-up-alien phase for laughs at a later date. To avoid some of this, maybe skip the two-day old professional photo shoot to let the baby adjust to life outside the womb by unshriveling and adopting humanoid features (depending on the level of alien you currently have). Once the baby has transitioned out of that #prunelife, then you are ready to start documenting! But should you enjoy comedy, by all means book the photo shoot on day one.

You'll need certain elements to achieve highest level newborn photos:

1. A white background so the baby really "pops."
2. Lots of light. Natural light tends to work best to show wrinkles and folds.
3. Baskets. Because babies and tomatoes look best in baskets.
4. Bows and knit caps. Summer weather be damned, babies get cold.
5. Baby positioned doing "grown up" tasks. Who's Daddy's little accountant?
6. Bare bottoms. Get 'em before modesty does.
7. Props that scream you and your spouse. Really imprint on that alien! Yankees hat, anybody?

Now let's say you waited a sufficient amount of time to let the baby "cuten up" for its official photogenic debut. Or maybe you didn't. Either way, the secret to grabbing the best newborn pictures is *sleep*! The more unconscious, the cuter the picture. Don't believe me?! Look at the complete work of Anne Geddes, the photographer who mastered the newborn photo shoot. Unconscious. All of 'em.

A sleeping baby doesn't mind being stuffed into a flowerpot, hammock, or some other not-actually-intended-for-a-baby contraption. And don't skimp on props! You can't forget props! The bigger the hair bow, the closer to heaven. Got a spare turkey laying around, stuff 'em in there. A sleeping baby will pose wherever and however you want.

#6. THE NURSING/BABY FORMULA DEBATE (SEE ALSO: THE MOST RIDICULOUS DEBATE EVER)

From the time we get the baby home (and even before), we, as dutiful modern mothers, have done the exhaustive research about how best to feed our newborn bundles of poop-making joy. The pressure to breastfeed is pervasive and continues to be a hot button issue. "I want to be a good mother, therefore, I must breastfeed." Women frequently have come to my site commenting that they don't want to nurse or cannot, but they feel like they should because of the pressure. After all, "breast is best" does not leave a lot of room for alternatives. If something is "best," all the other options must be less-than. Breastfeeding is another case of expectations and reality being a mismatched setup for new moms.

When I had my son, I had a lactation nurse in the hospital who was beyond mean. She tightly squeezed my breast and forced it into my son's mouth, a feeling I never forgot. She made me feel like a failure before I even started—not enough milk, not good enough milk, and so forth. The next day, I attended the lactation class offered by the hospital, which was only slightly better. All of the moms were at least struggling together. There was strength in our community as we all looked around at each other with questioning glances and trepidation. My son ended up needing formula (and a bottle!) during the hospital stay, and I told myself this was all going to be a spectacular failure, and the failure was all mine.

Once my son and I came home from the hospital, I was on a mission to nurse and feed him by any means necessary. I was not going to "fail" at breastfeeding. No formula. No nipple confusion by introducing those "evil bottles" into the equation. We were going to work at it and do this nursing thing. That lasted a very short time; we were using bottles after a few days.

Because of my postpartum anxiety, I became obsessed with how much milk he was receiving so I began pumping and nursing and documenting everything. Being able to see the quantities of milk in the bottle actually quelled my concerns but added new ones about nipple confusion. When the baby was three months old, we took a trip. For whatever crazy reason, I was worried about nursing him on the plane in public (silly, right?) so we introduced formula again (for the first time since those very early hospital days). He took to it like a natural, and he didn't explode or grow a second head. (I should pause to mention that my breasts were like *rocks* after the flight because I didn't nurse, and it was the longest time I had gone without expressing milk. Owwie! I DO NOT RECOMMEND! I lacked the confidence to nurse in public. Don't be like me. Invest in a cover-up or an old t-shirt or just whip 'em out.)

Long story short, my breastfeeding journey from my disappointing "failure" in the hospital to crazed pumper to formula mama to using all three was not at all what that lactation nurse would have recommended (or approved of) for me. Ironically, after all those ups and downs, my son continued nursing until he was two and a half years old because he loved the bonding (and the milk), and by then, it was a breeze. He'd probably still nurse to this very day if he had his druthers.

Don't be shy to switch to formula or pump into bottles or do a combination of all three. Maybe you thought you would be able to feed a village with those boobies, but they just weren't built for that! A fed baby is actually the "best" baby, even if breast milk is a wonder-beverage. Don't lose sight of that, and don't judge yourself on how the milk/formula gets in there because that's sanctimommy sh*t, and I already told you at the start of this book, no sanctimommies allowed.

Here are some of the "breast" resources:

* www.lllusa.org—LaLeche League USA offers resources for nursing mothers.
* www.breastfeeding-magazine.com—Online magazine for well, you know.
* www.cdc.gov/breastfeeding—The Center for Disease Control provides facts, figures, and resources on breastfeeding.

Pop Quiz:

*Circle the correct number of f*cks you should give about whether you nurse or use a bottle.*

> *0   1   5   10*

Answer: 0

Circle the correct number of f*cks you should give about feeding your baby breast milk versus formula.

0   1   5   10

Answer: 0

#7. RAPID FIRE ADVICE FOR NEW MOMS FROM @MODERNMOMPROBS INSTAGRAM FOLLOWERS

Ok, let's take a little break from the soapbox. Welcome to the digital village, Mama. Many of my followers wanted to share their advice with you. So here it goes, in no particular order:

* Don't be ashamed to ask for help from your partners, your family, and friends.
* Listen to your gut. No one knows your baby or your body like you do.
* You can't hold your baby too long.
* Just roll with it. It's all hard.
* Don't beat yourself up.
* Listen to people's advice, but don't take it all.
* Get sleep, let your pride go, accept help, and pay attention to your mental health.
* Have formula at home just in case, even if you plan to breastfeed.
* Be flexible.
* Don't over-Google, seriously. Don't.
* 80/20 rule: 80 percent of the time do your best; 20 percent do what gets you by.
* Despite what you see online, no one has the perfect, eating, sleeping baby.

* Order takeout.
* Don't buy every new gadget you see. You won't use it. I promise!
* Take in every moment. It really does go so fast, even if it doesn't seem like it now.
* Learn to be spontaneous and just go with what happens.
* It's ok to hate the newborn phase. It doesn't make you a bad mother or a terrible person.
* Determine boundaries and maintain them.
* Build your village (find other non-judgmental parents)!
* There is no shame in seeking professional help if you don't feel like yourself anymore.
* Take the damn shower and don't rush yourself out of it.
* Be kind to yourself. You are doing AWESOME!

THE ADVICE VENN

RUNNING OUT OF IDEAS FOR "A NEW MOM'S ADVICE" CHAPTER

ASKING YOUR INSTAGRAM FOLLOWERS TO WRITE IT FOR YOU

THIS CHAPTER

#8. Postpartum Depression, Blues, and General "WTF Is Going on Here?"

Bright sunny pictures. Babies in flowerpots. Smiling mothers doting on their precious smiling cherubs. Our eyes consume the pretty pictures of new motherhood leaving us to think, "Having a baby is easy and beautiful, and it will come completely naturally to me. My body is healed the second I give birth, and I will bask in the glory that is my newfound motherhood." For some (maybe most?) mothers, this simply is not true.

According to 2020mom.org, up to one in seven women will experience clinical depression during pregnancy or after birth. Maternal mental health issues can manifest as depression in some women and rage in others. For me, since I'm more prone to anxiety than depression, my issues presented as rage, like snapping at my husband for hosting Christmas dinner at our apartment four weeks after my baby was born. Or on a different occasion, going on a tirade where all I could say was "I can't even. I just can't even." Can't even what?! Who knows? I couldn't even find the words to complete my thoughts.

Maternal mental health disorder signs may include*:

* Loss of appetite
* Sadness
* Feelings of hopeless, helplessness, guilt, or despair
* Feeling inadequate as a mother
* Lack of interest in family and friends
* Obsessing over baby's safety
* Excessive worry
* Mental fog

---

* from 2020mom.org

* Difficulty in focusing
* Easily irritated or angry
* Trouble falling asleep or sleeping too much
* Feeling like you may want to harm the baby or yourself

New motherhood is exhausting and can make you feel like your brain is on fire. However, it's crucial to reflect on your feelings, behaviors, and moods. If these symptoms last longer than two weeks and intensify to the point of it affecting your quality of life, then you may be seeing signs of something more severe than the baby blues, which typically last about two weeks. Making this distinction between the baby blues and postpartum depression may help you to seek out the appropriate treatment.

You are not alone in this. Seek help if you don't feel like yourself. If you are expressing suicidal or dangerous thoughts, contact the National Suicide Prevention Lifeline (1-800-273-TALK).

To explore more about maternal mental health issues, check out:
* www.2020mom.org—2020 Mom leads the conversation about maternal mental health issues.
* www.thebluedotproject.org—The Blue Dot Project campaign fosters maternal mental health survivor-ship, support, and solidarity.
* www.postpartum.net—Postpartum Support International offers a hotline for non-emergency perinatal mental help issues (1-800-944-4773).

WHAT NEW MOTHERHOOD MAY LOOK LIKE

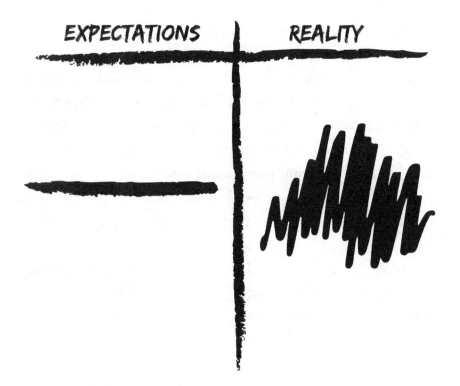

EXPECTATIONS | REALITY

#9. Infertility and Pregnancy Losses: It's So Hard and Nobody Talks about It

My son is a rainbow baby. If I would have called him that when he was born in 2012, no one would have known what I was talking about. A rainbow baby is a baby born after prior miscarriage(s). Like a rainbow following a storm.

Rainbow baby is a beautiful phrase that I wish existed back then because it would have made my losses slightly easier to cope with and understand, if I could think that maybe a rainbow was in my future. The problem is, no one really talks about loss, even though it is very, very common.

My journey to motherhood was not at all what I thought it would be (expectations messing with me again). In fact, it was more like a three-year-long, ultra-marathon or a blizzardy climb up Mount Everest, crying the whole way. I suffered three miscarriages, had two D&Cs (dilation and curettage), a polyp removal, and then infertility treatment requiring IUI (intrauterine insemination) procedures before our son was born. Even though time has passed, it is still so painful and raw to talk or write about. Ironically, in the modern world, it's easier to share my story with complete strangers than it ever was with my friends and family.

At one point, my husband and I thought about giving up, and really, we did. Then we talked about adopting. Then about being a consciously childless couple. For sure, we took some long breaks, especially after the second and third losses. Every pregnant friend I saw on Facebook or any friend who accidentally got pregnant made me green with envy and made us both very sad. "Why not us?!" But we kept going because we wanted a family. And one day, it finally worked.

My best friend recently reminded me that there must have been a reason for our pushing through—creating @modernmomprobs to help other women in the same situation. Back in 2009, I wished I had support either online or in real life to help me through the losses. But miscarriage is still such a taboo subject and source of shame for some reason. No one wants to touch it. Now I can confidently say:

I HAD A MISCARRIAGE.

It was horrendous, soul-wrenching, and a seemingly endless heartache. But we made it through to the other side. My suggestion if you suffered a miscarriage is to talk about it. I know it rips your soul out of your body to do so. Get it off your chest. Put it out to the universe because you never know who else you may help or who may be able to help you. One in four women experience pregnancy loss, and it's time we normalize the conversation.

Resources related to pregnancy loss:
* www.nationalshare.org—Share Pregnancy and Infant Loss Support is a community that offers support and group meetings.
* www.marchofdimes.org—The March of Dimes offers resources on health-related issues affecting pregnancy and infants.
* Read *I Had a Miscarriage: A Memoir, a Movement* by Jessica Zucker.

#10. LAUGH-PEEING YOUR WAY THROUGH LIFE: PELVIC HEALTH

Remember jumping on the trampoline as a carefree child? Your hair bouncing up and softly floating down, your smile stretching from ear to ear, your giggles echoing through the yard. Good memories. These days, if you jump on a trampoline, it goes like this, "Oh, sh*t! I peed!"

If you have been pregnant at some point, you may have a weakened pelvic floor, which may result in incontinence (i.e., you pee yourself) and/or discomfort during sex or urination.

Alright, ladies, assume the Kegel position and let's talk about some situations you now have to consider (reconsider?) after you had a kid.

* Trampolines (see above)
* Being a catcher on the softball team
* Checking to see what's under tables and chairs
* Going to Tina Fey movies or watching kids hit whiffle balls into their dads' groins
* Dusting (if it makes you cough or sneeze)
* Long car trips
* Running
* Olympic deadlift or power squatting events

If you tinkle a little when your bestie tells you about the time she apologized aloud for bumping into a mannequin at the department store, then maybe you should see a doctor specializing in pelvic health. There are things you can do, and if you haven't gotten my drift already in this book: don't be shy and do *ask for help*!

Loads of exercises exist to tighten your pelvic floor muscles from Kegel exercises to squats or yoga. One of my favorites is a hip thrust exercise we practiced in my Barre classes:

* *Lie on the floor.*
* *Bend your knees and place your feet firmly on the floor, keeping your knees in line with your hips.*
* *Tighten your pelvic floor muscles and push your hips up off the floor toward the ceiling while maintaining a straight back.*
* *Try not to pee.*
* *Hold this position for ten seconds and release.*
* *Repeat.*
* *Try not to pee.*

#11. Fingernails = Baby Werewolf Claws

I admit, I was underprepared for the razor-sharp werewolf claws of a newborn baby and the intricate process a new parent has to embark upon to clip them. Clipping your baby's nails is like defusing a bomb. It requires a calm temperament, excellent vision, and a steady hand. Who are we kidding? Robots actually defuse bombs now, so that task may be easier. C'mon, MIT, where's our "baby nail clipper" robot?

Since there's no such robot in production yet, the task still falls on us, the clipping-reluctant parents. But you have to do it. These suckers grow fast, and they can cause lots of damage! Here are some tips on how to nail the process (pun totally intended):

1. Use a *baby* nail clipper. The adult kinds will not do it. Hold your baby's finger, pressing the fingertip pad down and away from the nail. Gently clip, following the natural curve of the fingernail, making sure you don't go too low. You can use an emery board to file nails down a bit first. Stay away from using a metal nail file. It's too tough for their delicate nails. When doing toes, cut nails straight across. Luckily, their tootsies grow more slowly and require less frequent clipping.

2. Clip while sleeping. That's only if they are sleeping hard enough like they did during their newborn photo shoot in the flowerpot. If that's not possible, see number three.

3. Distract. Distract. Distract. Sing a song. Make funny faces. Practice your breathing exercises. You can do this!

4. And if you can't, seek help. Ask your partner, your aunt, your sister, your pediatrician. Just don't let anyone chew the baby's nails because germs can spread, and chewing leaves a

jagged edge. (Side note: My husband clipped our son's nails until he was two years old. I was too scared. Sometimes, confidence takes time!)

5. If all else fails, put on the mittens. Use baby socks or mittens to save newborns from their werewolf-selves. Covering the hands prevents newborns from scratching themselves in between nail-clipping sessions.

Take a deep breath. Don't stress! Defusing this bomb gets easier over time because their adorable werewolf claws grow, making the nail easier to reach, plus your skill level and confidence improves.

#12. BABY PROOFING: THE GREAT PARENTING ARMS RACE

In babyproofing, as in life, there are things we can control and things we cannot. Either way, all of these things will cause your mom anxiety to elevate to new heights. And good, that means you care about keeping that baby safe and out of the ER.

This is a sweeping overview of those things you can control, with a little about those things you cannot. Remember, this is an arms race. One week, you have a safe house capable of containing even the most daredevil of toddlers. A week later, they grow an inch taller, and now they can reach the knives!

Battlefronts:

* The Floor. Let's start where the babies live: down there. Stuff falls down. Baby eats stuff. Baby gets sick. Keep your gosh darned floor *clean* and free of choking hazards.
* Outlets. Oh, that little hole in the wall looks fun! Lemme grab the bobby pin that fell out of Grandma's hair (see "The

Floor") and stick it in there instead of our mouths. This is babyproofing 101. Go online and buy way more plug covers than you could ever possibly need, and fast.

* Windows. Live six inches above the ground? Sure you do, so that means falling out of a window would be bad. Lock those windows and don't let windows ever serve as a wall up against which toys or any leaning of any kind are encouraged. They're made of *glass*, and you can fall out of them. Windows are see-through death. Also, keep an eye out for window blinds, which can have tangly strings.

* Stairs. Baby gates are a must, no matter how many stairs you have. I have seen toddlers eat it on one small step. Those basement stairs are calling to that toddler of yours, and she will heed the call. Oh, the stairs are carpeted, you say? Ok, you tumble down them and tell me how that feels. Get a gate; there are so many easy options out there, just be sure to double check for recalls.

* Doors. Don't want a baby getting into that room full of power tools, archery equipment, and lawn fertilizer? Smart. Let's talk about doorknobs then. Your baby may not be smart enough to say "dada" yet, but they've watched you come in and out of that tool shed a million times, and they're wondering what hammers do. Lock it down like the Pentagon. I guarantee they've figured out the doorknob by now (like the velociraptors in *Jurassic Park*). Turn knobs will buy you slightly more time than the pull-down door handles…slightly.

* Corners of everything. Oh, the little guy is getting tall now? How cute he is, toddling around—right into the corners of literally everything. Specially made padding, blankets, pillows, whatever you gotta do. Eyes only come in pairs, and

replacements aren't cheap! Get on your knees, crawl around, and imagine all the stuff that could take you out if you ran full speed with your eyes closed (they basically do).

* Fireplaces. Hot and surrounded by hard stone. You know what to do....

* Water. Too hot, too cold, or too much. Never, ever, take your eyes off of a kid near water. Whether it's a pool, a bathtub, or a cup of water, there are too many tragedies every year to let your guard down.

* Cabinets and Drawers. Hide the knives because little Cutie wants them. And she shall find them if you don't install some cabinet safety. My son used to rattle the cabinet under the sink every day, as if to say, "I'll get in there one day, and I will eat everything in there." Tide pods look yummy when you're a baby. Purchase cabinet locks or even use rubber bands to keep your littles out of the dish detergent.

* Bathrooms. Slippery tile, baths, toilets, lots of pills, and cleaning stuff to eat. Best to just lock those rooms down as if they are full of fireworks and the baby is the match. By doing this, you will also save yourself a mess of toilet paper and water when baby decides to go fishing in the toilet.

* Wires. Husbands love to do some cord management. This is their time to shine. If you have a husband, make him organize that stuff and keep those electrons where they belong, inside the wires and not coursing through your kid's veins.

* Cribs. Cribs are expensive, but they are safer than ever. Within your budget, make sure you buy the safest crib you can find, follow the rules promoted by the American Academy of Pediatrics regarding safe sleep, and remember, Back is Best.

* Furniture. Secure any large furniture, like dressers, book-shelves, or TV stands to a solid wall. TVs and bureaus are heavy AF. Babies are not. But babies are strong and will tip these things over.
* Things you cannot control that will also F up your sh*t:
* Gravity. It's everywhere. Everywhere. Sucking your dear child's head into the earth. Stay low and slow.
* The Sun. Babies get sunburned very easily. Get some baby safe sunscreen if you're a big stroller nut like I was when our son was little. Those little legs will burn easily when exposed.
* Wind. An invisible force that will knock your child over and off of things, aided by gravity.

DIAGRAM: BEHAVIOR WHEN DANGEROUS ITEMS ARE PRESENT

ADULTS   TODDLERS

#13. Baby Burritos Are Delish: Swaddling Your Baby

If you're a mom in the twenty-first century, chances are you received swaddle cloths as a baby gift. They are ultra-soft and cute with delicate little elephants and foxes on them. So precious! But *how* do we use them?! If you're anything like me, I used them for *everything*—to wipe baby spit up, to line the bassinet, as a nursing cover both for my boobs and to cover my baby's head from falling crumbs while I scarfed down dinner. Ideally, they are used as swaddling cloths to wrap your bundle of joy into just that—a bundle.

In his book, *The Happiest Baby on the Block*, Dr. Harvey Karp recommends swaddling babies to replicate life in the womb, restrict their flailing arms, and put the babies in their "calm zone." We are all about calm, happy babies! So how do we best make a baby burrito? Easy peasy, lemon squeezy. Save yourself the trouble.

My suggestion: buy a wearable blanket (check out SwaddleMe adjustable wrap) or a sleep sack (Halo Sleep makes great ones). I *love* the Miracle Blanket which keeps little Houdini arms in the swaddle.

Use the swaddle cloths for *everything* else. One could probably write an entire book on their applications!

Remember to reduce the risk of SIDS, keep all stuffed animals, bumpers, loose bedding, and blankets out of cribs.

If you still prefer a do-it-yourself swaddle, here's a step by step guide:

Step 1: Find a flat surface.

Spread your baby's swaddle blanket out in the shape of a diamond. Fold the top corner down about six inches.

Step 2: Place your baby face-up on the blanket.

Her head should sit above the folded edge of the blanket.

Step 3: Straighten your baby's left arm.

Then take the left side of the blanket and wrap it over her left arm and chest. Tuck the blanket underneath her right arm and her back.

Step 4: Bring up the bottom.

Fold the bottom corner of the blanket up over your baby's body and tuck it under the first fold, under her chin. Straighten your baby's right arm and pull the right side of the blanket over your baby's body and tuck it under her left side.

Step 5: Secure the blanket.

Loosely twist the bottom of the blanket and tuck it underneath your baby.

Step 6: Observe the Reverse-Houdini.

Watch as your baby escapes from your poorly constructed swaddle contraption.

Step 7: Repeat Process.

Plan to be disappointed yet again.

Step 8: Go online and buy the stuff I already told you to buy earlier in this chapter!

#14. WAVE YOUR HANDS IN THE AIR LIKE YOU JUST DON'T CARE: BABY-WEARING

Party people! Put your hands in the air! And if you're *wearing* your baby, you can. Using a baby carrier, such as a Baby Bjorn, an Ergo Baby, or a Moby wrap, allows you to go about your business hands-free while Wrinkle McWrinkleface is strapped to your chest. This allows your baby to feel close to you with skin-to-skin contact, nap comfortably, and mellows her mood. With a little practice, you can even breastfeed with the baby in the carrier, especially with the inward-facing Ergobaby. I remember many days resting against a wall while my baby napped in his carrier. We used the Ergobaby so often, it became a new appendage. We walked *miles* in that carrier and it was the best.

When practicing baby-wearing, follow the T.I.C.K.S. guidelines to keep your baby close and safe:

* T: Tight. (The carrier should be as tight as comfortable to prevent falls.)
* I: In view at all times. (You should be able to see the baby's face by gazing down.)
* C: Close enough to kiss. (The baby's head should be close enough to your chin that you can easily give a smooch, and you'll want to anyway.)
* K: Keep chin off chest. (The baby's chin should not be curled down, which could restrict breathing.)
* S: Supported back. (Make sure the baby's back is in a natural position and her bottom is supported appropriately.)

(Based on guidelines from the UK Sling Consortium.)

Make sure the carrier is comfortable on your body also to prevent any back issues. And wear clothes a bit lighter than you would otherwise plan to, given the weather. It can get hot with ten pounds of sweetness strapped to your chest.

With the right carrier positioned properly, you can go food shopping, fold laundry, or walk through the park. The possibilities are practically endless. Maybe save rock climbing or mountain biking for when you're not wearing your infant. Just sayin'.

#15. Potty Training...in a Weekend?

Ok, here's one of those topics that brings moms anxiety across the planet. How? When? Where? Will it ever happen? First things first, deep breath. Look at the people you know or have known. Most of these barely functional adults have one life skill down pat, and it is the ability to toilet independently. At least it appears that way. So just remember, your kid will eventually make a boom boom in the elephant potty you bought them.

The Mayo Clinic page on potty training says that kids start to potty train anywhere from eighteen to thirty-six months old. One key statement on that page is, "There's no rush. If you start too early, it might take longer to train your child." This is so key! Equally key is knowing that this is largely a physical process that has nothing to do with how cooperative or smart they are. When they're ready mentally and physically, then they're ready. Stay positive and supportive. This is hard for them, too.

But what does "ready" look like? Here are some questions you should be answering "yes" to in order to determine readiness:

* Can your child walk to and sit on a toilet?
* Does your child show interest in the process of toileting (do they watch you)?
* Can your child pull down his or her pants and pull them up again?
* Can your child stay dry for up to two hours?
* Can your child understand and follow basic directions?
* Can your child communicate when he or she needs to go?
* Does your child seem interested in using the toilet or wearing "big-kid" underwear?

Once you establish readiness, it's time to get it going. As this is a book full of parenting advice by me, but also largely researched and crowdsourced, I will say there are way too many "methods" of potty training for me to be able to describe or speak to them all. Let me simply tell you what worked for us.

The Potty-Training Equation:
Three-day weekend + Zero pants + One package of Lysol wipes = One potty-trained toddler

Becky Mansfield wrote this great book, *Potty Train in a Weekend,* and it was a godsend. The long and the short of this method is get rid of the diapers in exchange for undies, feed that kid a ton of water, and just get them to sit down on the potty every hour or so until they put two and two together. We followed it to a tee, hunkered down for a weekend (pre-COVID this was a big deal), and by Monday our boy was peeing and pooping in the potty at least 80 percent of the time. He also enjoyed not wearing pants for the entire weekend and started to understand that he could just walk over to the potty when he wanted to, and I think he liked the independence aspect. We had a handful of setbacks, and once we did need to repeat the weekend full court press again. But after that, he got his sphincters under control, and we started carrying fewer diapers and wipes everywhere we went. We barely had to hose down the living room during the process, so I'll consider that a success.

Chapter 2
SLEEP PROBS

*A*mong mothers, there may be no two greater unifying forces than your own sleep deprivation and your kids' sleep disturbances. Ah, our little ones. When they're newborns, we're up nursing them, bottle feeding them, or listening to their breathing like FBI agents on a sting operation. As they grow, we're confronted with wandering lurkers at the foot of our beds, terrified victims of closet monsters, and Niagara Falls-level bed soakers. And every time we think we got it, here comes good ol' sleep regression to keep you on your toes and reset the clock. If you do get a rare Saturday to sleep in, you may even wake up to the smell of burning pancakes and the sound of smoke alarms going off (it's sad, Hubby tried so hard). So, let's rejoice in this thing we know so little about: sleep.

#16. CRY IT OUT (MOTHERF***ER)

Whether their cries fall on your deaf ears or you jump up like the house is on fire when you hear their shrieks, at some point you will need sleep. And that means a certain somebody's about to cry it the F out.

When my son was ten weeks old, I realized my brain was on fire from sleep deprivation. Actual fire. I could feel the flames dancing inside my skull. Three-hour bursts of sleep were a welcome relief early on, but I was getting weary. So, my husband and I gathered ourselves and made our first attempt to let the little guy "cry it out." And cry it out he did.

At 9:09 PM that fateful night, as we left his room, my husband and I high-fived and said, "This is the beginning of our new lives. We're going to sleep right now, and if he wakes up, so be it. He's not the boss of us." We got a pep talk from a trusted friend that if you just let them cry for ten minutes, they tire out and then after that, they just sleep. It was so easy, the solution was there for us the entire time. Baaa, we were first time parents, so silly, so naive.

At 9:15 PM, our son was fast asleep. Later than intended, but asleep nonetheless. We sat in bed, thinking it was some sort of trick, but no, we did it. By 9:30, we were asleep. At 10:45, after seventy-five minutes of glorious slumber, a whimper from the baby monitor. Meh, he's just rolling around. 10:47, another whimper. 10:49, a cry so loud and so forceful, every neighbor on the floors above and below our apartment must have been awakened. By 11:15, when we couldn't take it any longer, we grabbed our son and brought him back into our room.

He looked so sad. We were terrible parents to do this, right? He wasn't hungry, he wasn't wet, a bear had not attacked him, and he was now quiet as a lamb. We told ourselves he needed us, and we needed him. He'll sleep through the night when he's ready.

This insane self-talk would go on for several more days, at which point we realized this mushy bundle of joy was about as manipulative as your mother-in-law saying she's happy for you to host

Thanksgiving dinner. Four weeks later, after scouring the internet and talking to anybody who would listen, we stumbled upon the book, *Twelve Hours' Sleep by Twelve Weeks Old: A Step-by-Step Plan for Baby Sleep Success* by Suzy Giordano. We couldn't do the method to a tee, but let me tell you, we did get our lives back and started sleeping in six to eight hour stretches…for a while. So when you are ready, and when the baby is ready, get your sleep back. You need it.

#17. YOUR FIRST COMPLETE NIGHT'S SLEEP (AND PHILOSOPHY 101)

A little tangent here. If you've ever taken a philosophy class, you've encountered the works of John Stuart Mill. Some have said he's one of the most influential philosophers in history, so he's sort of a big deal. See, our boy JSM was a Utilitarian, concerned with all matters of "greatest good". He argued that intellectual and moral pleasures are superior to more physical forms of pleasure. So, let me tell you how wrong this guy was.

THE MOM EARTHLY PLEASURES PYRAMID

BABY'S FIRST FULL NIGHT'S SLEEP

UNINTERRUPTED SHOWER

SEX

ICE CREAM

CAFFEINE

Talk all you will about wonderful meals, great sex, amazing works of art, and even higher intellectual pleasures. All are complete *trash* compared to the first night of sleep I got after three months of the all-out war on my brain. So, I present to you a proper representation of earthly mom pleasures in the figure below, lest you think you should go without:

So yeah, you need to work on getting that first good night's sleep. And now! Also, seriously John Stuart Mill, did you not have kids?

#18. Sleep Regression: Going Forward in Reverse

Mike Tyson once said, "Everybody has a plan until they get punched in the mouth." And that, my friends, is the best-known description of sleep regression.

Sleep deprivation is a marathon. In some ways, by the time you're nearing the end, you don't even feel the pain anymore. But that is mostly because you have been practice-running that marathon for a long while leading up to the race. Sleep regression is like lying on the couch for six months and then being forced to run 26.2 miles at gunpoint. It hurts really badly!

The "why" of sleep regression is often a mystery, but here's what we know. All of your old tricks and powers are now useless. If you do not adapt, you will die. And if you don't have a death wish, I recommend the book *Healthy Sleep Habits, Happy Child, 4th Edition: A Step-by-Step Program for a Good Night's Sleep* by Marc Weissbluth, MD.

The Sleep Stability Graph

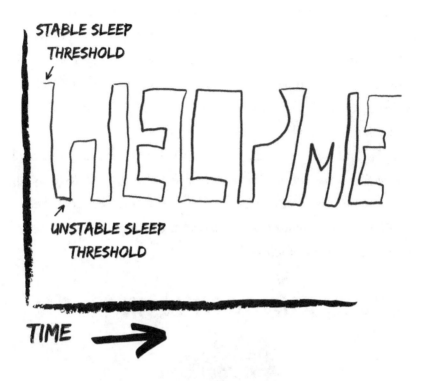

#19. Co-Sleeping Like a Boss

Ah, co-sleeping. This popular topic is almost as controversial as breastfeeding. In one corner, parents contend that it builds trust and creates a bond. In the other corner, parents are sick of being kicked in the head by their three-year-old "octopus." Speaking of corners, that is where most co-sleeping parents end up. On the corner of their bed. Falling-off-limbs-dangling-crick-in-the-neck-getting-kicked-in-the-kidneys-sleeping is the full name for co-sleeping (little known fact). I don't have to tell you it's not the most conducive, beneficial way to sleep night after night.

Think your little one is too small to commandeer an entire bed? It's a fact that once a child co-sleeps with his parents, he will commence starfish configuration. What is starfish configuration? Good question. This phenomenon occurs when the child stretches his arms and legs into an immovable starfish-like position. (See illustration.) Good luck getting some sleep with your child in this position! There's always the couch for you. Or better yet, pick him up and gently place him back in his *own* bed.

For more habitual sleep issues, I highly recommend the book *Putting Sleep Problems to Bed: Solutions for Children Ages 0-18* by Dr. Lisa Medalie and Professor David Gozal. It offers sleep logs, behavior charts, and evidence-based behavioral treatment strategies to get those kiddos back in their beds again fast!

STARFISH CONFIGURATION

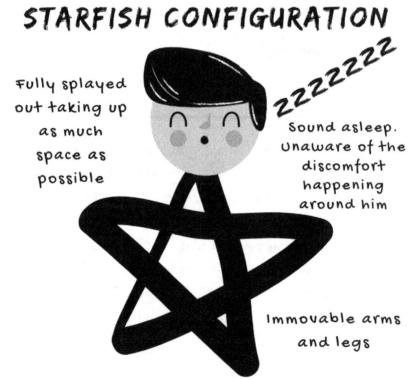

Fully splayed out taking up as much space as possible

zzzzzz

Sound asleep. Unaware of the discomfort happening around him

Immovable arms and legs

#20. The Crib to Bed Transition, or "The Call is Coming from INSIDE the House!!!"

The big boy/big girl bed is a rite of passage for kids and parents everywhere. It's that magical moment when the first bits of freedom and trust get expressed for a family. And it's a real circus.

Be forewarned, I have no tips or tricks for making this smooth, and I don't really know where to start with this life event. For us, it was nowhere near as bad as the crying it out phase. So I will just share a story and leave it there so you can decide when it's time to turn that safety cage you call a crib into a wide-open frenzy.

Some friends of ours converted the crib to a bed when their son was three years old. This was their first child, and he was a really well-behaved, adorable kid. The big boy bed was going to be a breeze. Let's just consider what happened on night one.

The boy got his usual bedtime routine. He was excited about his new digs, but he went down pretty easily and on time. He was generally a good sleeper up to that point, so they weren't expecting any premature wakeups or anything. The household was pretty well babyproofed. For all intents and purposes, this was a setup for success on every single level.

At 6:00 AM, the father woke up because usually, the little guy would have called for them by that time. But he didn't. So, Dad went straight into the boy's room and of course, he was nowhere to be found! Now, apartment living at least makes it easy to track down your kids when they aren't where you expect them to be, so it only took ten seconds to find the rascal.

He was passed out, sleeping upside down on the couch. He had taken his shirt off (sure). Next to him was a box of chocolate chip cookies (half-eaten), a bottle of mustard (why?), a family portrait (super cute), and his bottle. A kitchen chair had been pushed in front of the refrigerator, which was wide open, and *all* of the packets of baby food were scattered around on the floor in what must have been a feeble attempt to get them open. The sink was running. And some sort of sticky substance had been smeared on the windows in the living room.

Had he been planning this all along? Did the plan come together as it unfolded? Did he wake up and say, "I'm 'bout to mess sh*t up?" I think the answer to any of these questions is just proof that converting to the big kid bed is *no joke*. Hide the car keys. Up that baby-proofing game some more. And maybe just sleep a little lighter the first night or two because all of this is crazy, and all of it is true.

#21. Car Naps Are Pure Evil and Should be Outlawed

Here's a little math problem for you (yes, there are math problems in this book).

Your child needs exactly ten hours of sleep every night, and she takes a thirty-minute nap in the car on the way back from a party.

A) Assuming a usual bedtime of 8:00 PM, what will be her new bedtime?

B) How much sleep will she need/get on the night in question?

Go ahead, get a piece of scrap paper and work it out. We'll grade your work.

Answer to A: If you think the answer is she'll go to bed a little later at 8:30 PM and still get nine hours and thirty minutes, you are just wrong, wrong, wrong. The math on car naps does not follow the sort of number system you learned in school or encountered in real adult life. If your child takes a thirty-minute car nap, expect her to go to sleep two or three hours later than expected. Why? Nobody knows.

Answer to B: As for sleep duration, she will wake up at 5:30 AM. *Without fail.* Why? Also unknown. Take whatever the usual wakeup time is and just wind it back to 5:30. But wait, you say, that's only a few hours of sleep, and my kid needs ten full hours. Well, that's not how this works, my dear. Oh, they will also be a complete disaster the entire next day (or two).

So, if your spouse hits you with a plan that sounds something like this: "We'll go to your uncle's birthday and leave at 7:00 PM, and he can nap in the car on the way home," then good luck; your next forty-eight hours are gonna be a grind. And that is one hundred percent going to happen—the only math I am sure of.

#22. "OH THEY'RE GONNA BE SO TIRED AFTER THEY RUN AROUND LIKE THIS" AKA THE GREATEST LIE EVER TOLD

Here's another little yarn that grandparents, in particular, like to spin. It is likely they remember children this way because those parts of their memory have been repressed and warped over time so that they could go on with a normal life. But letting kids run around like crazy and to the point of exhaustion has zero correlation to being "tired out," let alone having a good night's sleep. They will *not* tire themselves out. There's no gas tank or energy meter to deplete and then parlay into sleep. I want to repeat this. They will *not* tire themselves out.

What you will have after a marathon of physical exertion and playtime is a sweaty, dirty, overtired ball of emotions who will have a tough time unwinding. Use all the lavender lotion you want, it ain't gonna work.

Here's an idea: next time, read the playdate section of this book (Prob #39) and cap that mess at two hours of full exertion, *max*. Past that, I make no guarantees. You made your bed. Leave the family party early, even if your aunt gives you guff for it. Go home. Stick to your regular sleep schedule. You will thank yourself in the morning.

THE "THEY WILL SLEEP WELL TONIGHT" CHART

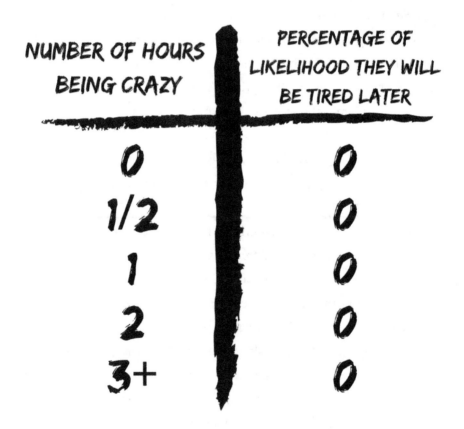

NUMBER OF HOURS BEING CRAZY	PERCENTAGE OF LIKELIHOOD THEY WILL BE TIRED LATER
0	0
1/2	0
1	0
2	0
3+	0

#23. Nightmares of Our Own Creation: Monsters and Tooth Fairies

Magical thinking is a hallmark of childhood. It's really adorable when the little ones think their teddy bears are alive, or that Santa is coming down the chimney, or that the tooth fairy is coming to put far too much money under their pillows. We play into a lot of this stuff as parents. So it should be no surprise that kids can let their imaginations get the best of them.

My son had a very consistent closet monster starting at the age of five. This did coincide with him losing his first tooth, but I'm not gonna blame the tooth fairy just yet on this one. Although, you have to admit that the idea that a magical fairy can just get into your room overnight while you're asleep opens up a world of monsters. My son had a very clear picture of how this monster looked, what it would do (eat him, of course), and it disrupted his sleep (but by age five you know that can happen at any time).

We tried everything we read to do. Keep bedtime light and happy. Monster. Talk it through during the day to make it less powerful. Monster. Nightlight. Monster.

We felt bad because it was clear nothing was working. Naturally, bedtime became a real struggle, and we were at a loss for how to help him. We tried an idea I came up with as a babysitter in my teen years: *monster spray*. I used to spritz monster spray from an invisible bottle to help my charge sleep peacefully, complete with my "sppiitss sppiitss" sound effect. (Funny story, the night after I babysat, the toddler asked her mother to use the monster spray, and Mom had *no* idea what she was talking about. Mom searched her entire house for my fictitious spray!) So I dusted the invisible bottle off of the proverbial shelf and gave it a few pumps. It actually was something he took to very well. Every night we would read a story, tuck him in, and spray a very dilute lavender spray on his sheets and by the closet. The monster went away. Sure it came back periodically, but the monster spray seemed to work each time. I should have patented it back in 1996.

Now the tooth fairy, that's another story. I will say this, though: Can we all agree that the max any tooth should be worth is one dollar?! When other kids tell my son the tooth fairy gave them a twenty-dollar bill, I'm just like, "Well there are many different tooth fairies, and ours just doesn't have that kind of budget." But c'mon. Twenty dollars? You're killin' me here.

#24. Blue Light from Hell: Screens versus Sleep

As hard as it is to peel your children away from their tablets or the TV before bedtime, it's important to set boundaries and pry the devices from their little hands. The blue light that comes from these screens can turn sleepy time into cray cray time! It delays the release of melatonin, increases alertness, and resets the body's circadian rhythm (the body's internal clock). Over time, this disruption can affect sleep quality, daytime productivity, and general well-being. Read: a hot mess!

According to the National Sleep Foundation:

"The reason that blue light is so problematic is that it has a short wavelength that affects levels of melatonin more than any other wavelength does. Light from fluorescent bulbs and LED lights can produce the same effect. Normally, the pineal gland in the brain begins to release melatonin a couple of hours before bedtime, and melatonin reaches its peak in the middle of the night. When people read on a blue light-emitting device (like a tablet, rather than from a printed book) in the evening, it takes them longer to fall asleep; plus, they tend to have less REM sleep (when dreams occur) and wake up feeling sleepier—even after eight hours of shuteye."

No one wants a tired, grumpy kid on their hands. You don't need a tour guide to tell you that!

Here's what I can tell you: impose a digital curfew in your house. Have your children power down their devices, including the TV, an hour or two before bedtime so their bodies can start producing more melatonin. If that's just not possible, dim the brightness on the screen. Or, install an app that warms up the colors on the screen to red hues. Using nightlights in the bedroom and the bathroom? Avoid using blue-hued bulbs (these tend to be the energy-efficient ones). Instead, opt for dim red lights because red light has a higher wavelength and does not suppress the release of melatonin.

The same goes for you, Mama. As tempting as it is to scroll Instagram at 1:00 AM, the blue light will not aid in sending you to Slumbertown.

Want to learn more? Check out:
* Sleepfoundation.org

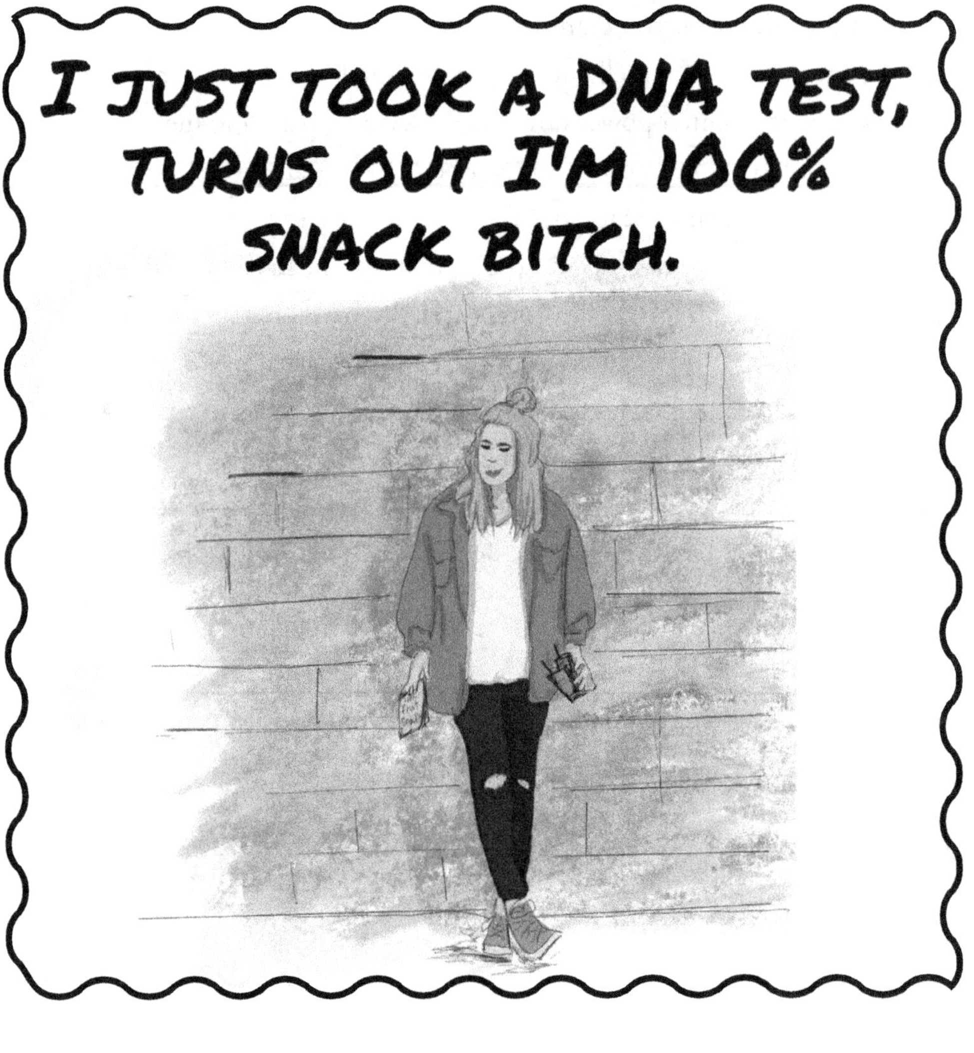
I JUST TOOK A DNA TEST,
TURNS OUT I'M 100%
SNACK BITCH.

Chapter 3
MEAL PROBS

*E*ating is one of the great pleasures of life—unless, of course, you're a mom. Kids don't want to stop what they are doing to eat. And you wish you could have just five minutes to eat. So start boiling some water for that special buttered pasta dish your little boo demands. We're gonna get saucy!

#25. HIGHCHAIRS AND THE MESSES THEREUNDER

Kids are cute, but they're pretty bad at eating. First, they can't figure out what to do when you shove the food in there. Then, once they figure it out, the food just goes everywhere. By the looks of the area under my husband's chair at the kitchen table, there isn't much hope for us, but you can still have a neat kitchen most of the time. Here are some helpful tips to mitigate the damage.

Bibs aren't just for lobster boils. But the classic cloth bib is sort of a waste when you have a kid that drops most of the food that they mean to eat. When a friend gifted us the food catcher pouch bib contraption, my first inclination was to say, "What is this monstrosity?" But let me tell you, looks aren't everything. Sure, these bibs don't usually say cute things like "Mommy's Little Winner," but they will catch those mashed sweet potatoes like a champ. Do yourself a favor: Google "bibs with food catcher" right now and start to get some floor space back. You're gonna be the one cleaning that mess, so you better get serious about preventative measures today.

When you are out of the highchair phase, your new life begins. Whether it's a mini kids table or a booster to the kitchen table or a real-life big girl chair, stuff's about to get wild. Kids do not respect the concept of eating over their plates, holding their silverware consistently or at all, and they certainly do not care if ants take refuge in the area beneath their chair. They also love to have buttery hands, so I hope the chairs are made of a fabric that wipes easily. Maybe stone? Just plan based on this description; you can thank me later.

So what's a mom to do? No, seriously, I'm asking *you* on this one because I don't even have a solution besides badgering them every night at dinner. So you know where to find me on Insta. Just let me know because we need help at home, ASAP.

Topsy-turvied you on this one, huh? Bet you weren't expecting that!

For People Who Don't Eat Much, Kids Sure Do Love To Compare Moms' Bodies To Food:

"Mom, your butt is like Jell-O."

"Your boobies are like pancakes."

"Your hair looks like spaghetti and meatballs."

"Your tummy is squishy like a marshmallow."

"Your breath smells like chocolate. Did you eat my Easter candy again?"

#26. THE PICKY EATER, A CHILD GOURMAND

Lots of kids (as many as 20 percent) will become selective eaters at some point in life. Almost all of them will grow out of it. So let's just get that out there and breathe a sigh of relief. Now, let's pick this stuff apart because it's frustrating AF!

A picky or selective eater is a kid who is unwilling to try new foods and who has strong food preferences. Can be considered a chop-buster, if you will.

Here's the picky eater food pyramid in case you're wondering:

THE PICKY EATER FOOD PYRAMID

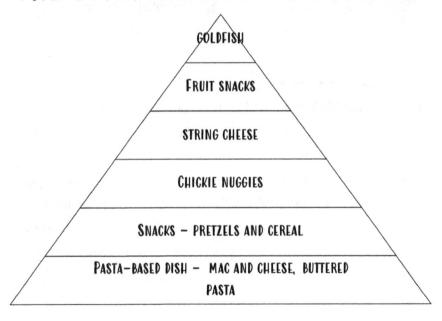

GOLDFISH

FRUIT SNACKS

STRING CHEESE

CHICKIE NUGGIES

SNACKS – PRETZELS AND CEREAL

PASTA-BASED DISH – MAC AND CHEESE, BUTTERED PASTA

So what's a mom to do?

1. Respect their appetites and realize a bag of pretzels can really fill up a little belly, so maybe your snack schedule is making it challenging.
2. Introduce new foods slowly and be patient.
3. Do your best to all eat the same meal rather than be a short order cook.
4. Engage your child, make it fun and creative.
5. Use good modeling by eating new things and healthy foods.
6. Minimize dinner table distractions.
7. Don't offer dessert as a reward.
8. Don't make every meal a fight or obsession. Trust that they likely will grow out of it, and as long as they are maintaining a healthy weight, they are probably ok. Talk with the pediatrician if you are worried.

#27. EATING ORGANIC-ISH

The road to Taco Bell is paved with good intentions. Any attempts at eating organic in our household have devolved since my son started eating solid foods. When my son was an infant, I made homemade baby food—peeling, slicing, and steaming those organic veggies myself. Now he eats goldfish crackers with the viciousness and ferocity of a shark. So there's that. The good news is, non-organic food (but not necessarily processed food) is generally just as safe and healthy for you and your family as organic food. Never mind that mom guilt part though; here are some pros and cons of eating organic:

Pros:
* Organic farming tends to be more friendly to the environment. I'm all about making friends with the environment.

* Organic food contains no hydrogenated fat. Heart healthy! Yum!

* Organic farming usually means that animals are fed a natural diet and kept in free-range conditions.

* Lower use of pesticides and antibiotics. Less chemicals seems good.

Cons:

* Organic food may spoil faster, so you better have those menus planned for the week.

* Expensive! You'd think something that got less stuff sprayed on it should cost less, but what do I know?

* Many studies have found that there are very few tangible health benefits to the most commonly purchased organic food.

* You may confuse organic with "eat as much of this as you want," but a steak is still a steak.

Organic meats, apples, berries, grapes, spinach, and milk are still my jam, though. I think they taste better, and apples and spinach seem to be the biggest offenders where chemical use is concerned in the non-organic realm. So that's that, and I gotta run because I don't wanna burn my cupcakes!

#28. Foods I Never Thought Would Pass As Dinner Until I Became a Parent

I'm going to level with you: at some point, you just have to get some calories in that little body of theirs so the next pediatrician visit doesn't end with them calling protective services. Here are some of the "meals" I have fed or am currently feeding my boy in order for him to survive and thrive. It's the culinary version of "Never Did I Ever."

1.   A plate of shredded cheese.

     Dairy is good, right? The major risk with this meal is the little shreds of cheese get everywhere, but it's a crowd pleaser and calorie-dense. Maybe you can work up to mac and cheese, little guy? Sheesh!

2.   Butter with some pasta sprinkled on top.

     What surprises me is that we eat this meal three times a week, every week. What doesn't surprise me is that we usually get distracted, eat four noodles, let the rest get cold, and then say it tastes gross now because it's cold. Try to make sure you have a fifty/fifty ratio of butter to pasta in order for this meal to be acceptable. Also, since you're always going to make too much pasta, save some for when the first batch gets too cold, eat that bowl yourself, and replace with the fresher stuff.

3.   Anything from an arcade or amusement park.

     I'm not proud of this, but all the loud noises and bright lights confuse the children into eating the microwaved pizza slices made by an animatronic mouse.

4.   Pretzels.

     Are pretzels dinner? I want to say "no," but hear me out on this one. You can dip them in a nut butter, and your kid will eat them until her tummy is full. Also, sometimes it's like, F@#$ it. Ya know? So yeah, pretzels can be dinner if you try hard enough and throw some carrots and almonds in there too. Ride that crunchy wave.

A few serious words. Try your kids' food yourself. Sometimes it's sh*t, and they don't want to eat it because it's sh*t. They have taste buds, too! My husband and I fed our son some new chickpea-based mac and cheese one time, and he would not eat it. We tried and tried to coax him and he was emphatic. So we tried it…totally inedible trash. They can't all be winners, so give your kids a little more credit.

If you are genuinely concerned your child is not eating healthily enough, always talk to your pediatrician. I guarantee you that nine out of ten times you will feel better when they admit kids are weirdos, and they just eat like weirdos.

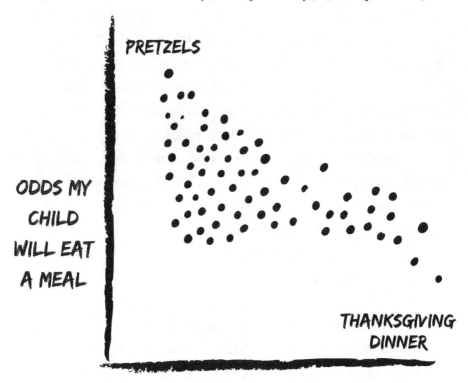

THE PICKY EATER SCATTERPLOT

PRETZELS

ODDS MY CHILD WILL EAT A MEAL

THANKSGIVING DINNER

TIME SPENT MAKING MEAL

#29. THE GREAT CHICKEN NUGGET DEBATE

I present to you the single most important chapter in this entire book: knowing which nuggets to get and when.

Chicken nuggets are the cornerstone of every school-age food pyramid. And if you aren't pilfering those cold, half-eaten nuggies they leave behind, you're missing out. Get on that, you're worth it.

As moms, we feed our families several meals a day, *every day*. For most of those meals, we have to cook, set the table, put the food on the table, coax everyone to eat, listen to everyone complain that "this is gross," clear the table, scrape the uneaten food off their plates, load the dishwasher, scrub the pots, and wipe down the countertops. Sometimes…just sometimes…we want to avoid this rigmarole. Sometimes we want to strap our loves into their car seats, crank our music, and cruise down the road to the drive-thru at the closest fast food restaurant. Fries taste better and soda tastes sweeter when the kids are strapped in wolfing down their nuggets.

Across these great United States, there are really three main competitors for drive-thru chicken nuggets. Chicken tenders are for more refined palettes, maybe the twelve-year-old in your car. But the little guys want nuggies. And nuggies they shall have.

While I cannot decide for you which nugget is best, this is how to approach the great nugget debate.

Burger King: Now, I am just gonna say, we live closest to a Burger King. So, if there were a loyalty card for BK, we'd already have it. My son thinks BK nuggets are the sh*t, and mommy gets a Coke Zero. Also, you put that little crown on their heads, and you're totally the best mom ever that night.

McDonald's: IMHO nothing makes your car smell as good as McDonald's. I think the fries are what does it. But the fact remains, the nuggies here are good, and they travel well. Pre-pandemic we'd even stay at the indoor play space for an hour while I had an iced coffee. Tear….

Wendy's: I don't know what it is about Wendy's. Clever marketing, maybe? But it always feels like it's a little bit fancier than the other fast food joints. The nuggets are nice and salty like the BK nuggets, flavorful like the McDonald's nuggets, and they keep me feeling classy. And the kid's meals toys are usually something to spark creativity!

And the winner is…whichever nugget I can get my hands on the fastest!

Do you enjoy fast food restaurants because…?

A. *They provide hot, delicious food.*

B. *They offer quality food at a fair price.*

C. *You can eat a hot meal while your children are strapped down in their car seats, and you can pump up the radio to listen to your fave songs while scarfing down deliciously salty fries in the parking lot.*

D. *All of the above.*

E. *Don't lie. We know the answer is C.*

#30. WELCOME TO CHILI'S: "EATING" IN RESTAURANTS

It's one of the true pleasures in the life of a couple. An elegant restaurant. Food you both enjoy. Maybe a cocktail. Since those days only exist in the abstract at this point, it is better to face life head-on and consider the extent to which you can enjoy dining out as a parent.

Babies lull you into a false sense of confidence on many things, and dining out is no exception. Sure, you may have to get over the hurdle of whipping a boob out in the middle of your favorite place, but you can still go, even if you occasionally cover the baby with some crumbs. As long as they're fed and watered, these cute little buggers will be totally fine in their car seat laid out on the booth. They may even fall asleep, and you and your significant other can chat it up.

But once you get to high-chair mode, sh*t is gonna get real. Here's an example. We went as a family to some destination, I can't remember where because I slept so little that my brain has no memories from the trip. Our son was thirteen months old. He liked to sit in his chair and fumble with his food or a toy. In this particular instance, he had a toy that he dropped under his chair. As it fell, he followed its path, slamming his forehead right into the table and needless to say, losing it. He was fine, no concussion, but he had an egg on his head immediately, and the entrees hadn't even come out. So that was quite a dinner.

Three- and four-year-olds love the dirty nether region that is Under-the-Table-Land. Why play with your Hot Wheels on top of the table when you can drive them through the dirty old food particles beneath you? Oh, and don't forget that being under a table means that you have to get up quickly all the time and hit your head on the underside of said table. This makes dinners really fun as you attempt to keep one hand on the moving noggin and another on the food. If the waiter doesn't seem to understand that you have a ticking time bomb sitting with you in the booth, you need to let them know. Order a basket of fries and the kid's meal before the drinks and prepare to do some competitive eating when your own food arrives.

You usually limit screen time, but you also would like to go back out to a restaurant now that your kid is five or six years old? Welp, life is about compromises, so let me endorse a place that has become our mainstay: Chili's. I don't care what you think, that little tablet thingy they have with the video games has allowed us to have dinner whenever we want and in relative peace. Don't fall for this whole "crayons and a placemat to color" nonsense. That will get you through the drink order and possibly the appetizers, but that's it. Screen time… for older kids…at least until their food arrives. Don't worry, they're gonna love you for it. Most importantly, you just got through an entire meal, and maybe you even felt like you were in control of your life for a bit.

#31. COOKING AS A FAMILY: BECAUSE THE KITCHEN LOOKED TOO CLEAN

Cooking as a family has many benefits. It's a relatively cheap way of bonding. It's a great way to foster communication and teamwork. And it can even teach some practical skills like measuring, following instructions, and like, how to survive if Mommy decides to join the circus one day. In theory, cooking is also a way to decrease some pickiness since it actively engages kids in the process of making their own meals.

But cooking with kids is also challenging and potentially dangerous if you are gullible enough to think they will not walk right into the oven. They will. Here are some tips for cooking together, without adding a side of baked visit-to-the-emergency-room.

* Provide kid-friendly supplies. Believe it or not, these exist. But before you decide to shell out a few bucks so they don't peel the skin off their fingers, know that simple stuff like measur-

ing some olive oil is a big ask for kids. Just use what you have, keep your expectations very low, and keep the dangerous stuff to yourself. Anything involving plastic should be fair game though, so let them have at it. Our son loves kneading and patting dough, pouring liquids of any sort, mixing things, and measuring. We thank him profusely for his help, and he walks around like he's Gordon Ramsay minus the foul language.

* Prepare for a huge mess so that you don't get upset or act surprised when the flour goes flying all over the kitchen. It's on you to pick meals that won't end up with marinara on the ceiling or beet juice on the tile. I would also prepare the kitchen as if you were preparing a soon-to-be crime scene. This way, after the mess happens, you can at least pick up those towels and newspaper and toss them. Like it never even happened.

* If your kids can read, have them practice reading aloud and leading the team by reading the recipe. They can assign roles, too, if they're up for it. It's ok to have some of the harder or more dangerous steps done beforehand. Most kids will feel victorious having washed a vegetable without your assistance. Let them read the recipe and assign some roles, and they'll think they created this recipe themselves.

* Pick recipes that they like. It's nice for them to understand how something as simple as pasta gets to their plate. But you should also consider how long the meal will take to cook. We have found that by the time we're done preparing a meal, my son is ready to eat, so keep the cooking times modest depending on how hungry and/or patient your children are. It's no use spending an hour cooking only to have to make some mac and cheese for the hungry brood waiting for the original meal to finish cooking.

* Take your time. Turn on some music. Make it fun. It's meant to be fun. And if it's looking like the meal is going to be *gross*, order a pizza. Everyone loves Pizza Night!

Some delish recipe sites include:
* www.gimmesomeoven.com
* www.simplyrecipes.com
* www.budgetbytes.com
* www.thepioneerwoman.com
* www.melskitchencafe.com

#32. Is It Dinner Time Again? A Chef's Work Never Ends.

If you are the primary chef in your household, please review this daily schedule. The day and month are unimportant, but this will sum up your culinary existence as a mom. Consider yourself the chef of a cruise ship bound for nowhere.

Time	Food-based Task	Notes
Midnight–6:00 AM	Sleep	Sleep is crucial. You will need energy to prepare meals
7:00 AM	Breakfast Prep	Make a cup of coffee. Note: you will forget you made the cup of coffee, so please re-heat coffee at 7:30 AM
8:00 AM	Breakfast encouragement for meandering children	You should again have a cup of coffee

9:00 AM–11:00 AM	Provision snacks	Consider more coffee (optional)
Noon	Lunch Prep/Lunch	
1:00 PM–4:00 PM	Provision snacks	Have fleeting thought regarding what to make for dinner later
5:00 PM	Panic about lack of dinner prep	This hour will sneak up on you and you will realize that nothing is thawed or that you are out of what you planned to make for dinner
6:00 PM	Dinner Prep	Whatever you got
7:00 PM	Planning tomorrow's dinner	Remind yourself you need to thaw some stuff for tomorrow's dinner
7:15 PM	Scroll Instagram	Note: You have now forgotten to prep for tomorrow's dinner
7:30 PM	Bath time and bedtime	
9:00 PM	Go to sleep	Think to yourself, there was something I wanted to do right after dinner. Forget what it was

#33. Why, Food Bloggers? WHY?!?

I don't consider myself a great cook. I have a few things I make really well, and I rarely get adventurous. But I like a nice new recipe every now and again. I'm just gonna put this out there: of all the progress we've made on various frontiers (e.g., modern medicine, computing technology, education), we have severely regressed as a society where cooking recipes are concerned.

It used to be your mom would get the idea to make something for you, and she'd grab that old dog-eared copy of *The Joy of Cooking* from the cabinet and boom, an hour later you'd have some awesome baked chicken. Nowadays, I have to sit through a fifteen-minute video of a food blogger talking about the seasons changing and the seasonality of the onions at the local farmer's market. So I pause that and then comb through the entire page just to get to the five-ingredient recipe that has three steps. That internet meme by Julie Burton really summed it up, "Just show me the recipe, food bloggers." Do yourself a favor. Always scroll to the bottom of the page!

CONTENT OF A FOOD BLOGGER'S WEBSITE

RECIPE

TALKING ABOUT FRESH INGREDIENTS AND INSPIRATION FOR THIS DISH

When your children try to make you laugh, *LAUGH*. They love to hear your laughter as much as you love to hear theirs.

Chapter 4
KID PROBS

The school years present a whole new set of unexpected problems for most moms. Growing up is hard for everybody, and things are getting more complicated by the day. Rules for school: be kind, be careful, be cool because you don't know how to do math anymore. Welcome to the school daze.

#34. Childhood Phases (Not According to Parenting Books).

Below are some developmental stages you will not read in Dr. Spock's parenting book or really any pediatrics manual on the planet. But this is the real sh*t.

0–1 year old: Survival Mode. They're gonna do all sorts of unpredictable sh*t this first year. They're a blob and then suddenly they aren't. Somewhere along the line they get vaccinations and also find their limbs, which they stick in their mouths. Diaper rash. Diarrhea. Sleep regression. Buckle up. Just survive!

2: Terrible Twos. Characterized by tantrums, screaming, general honey badger-like behavior and also, screaming; this phase has gotten a lot of historical attention and for good reason. Brain development is a really arduous process. Be kind and sympathetic; they're like little guppies surrounded by big people who make odd sounds and take them places. They don't know what to do with their little hands and feet now. Brain scramblies. Hitting other kids. Climbing out of cribs.

3: Threenager or Threenado. This phase is distinguished by similar features as the Terrible Twos plus increased vocabulary and sassiness. A particularly excellent age for ruining plans and succumbing to accidental injuries. See phase one, and just make it through!

4: "You Gotta Be F*cking Kidding Me" Fours. A child in this phase demonstrates reduced tantrums while acute sassiness is off the charts. The word "No" is used again and again by all parties involved, and having a "No" war is a daily occurrence. Rationality is forming, however, and the four-year-old can occasionally be talked off the proverbial ledge.

5–9: Easy Street. You got a real kid on your hands now; however, you may have to endure listening to stories about Minecraft, Pokémon, Roblox, and watching YouTubers. Meltdowns are still a thing, though; don't let anybody fool you.

10–12: Tweens. See extreme sassiness of four-year-olds coupled with a desire for independence because they're big shots now. Mmmhmmmm. Good luck, Mama, I was a terror at this phase. Weren't you?

13–19: Teenagers. That's another book altogether.

CHILDHOOD DEVELOPMENT TIMELINE

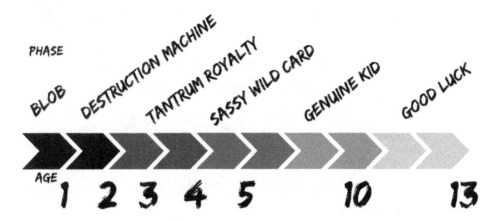

PHASE

BLOB

DESTRUCTION MACHINE

TANTRUM ROYALTY

SASSY WILD CARD

GENUINE KID

GOOD LUCK

AGE 1 2 3 4 5 10 13

#35. THE STRUCTURE AND FUNCTION OF A BIRTHDAY PARTY

The only way to survive the plethora of birthday parties you will attend (especially from ages three to eight) is to first understand how and why they exist. Knowledge is power, or something.

Functionally, a child's birthday party serves two purposes. First, it is a display to other parents that you respect and will perpetuate the understood social norms of your community, namely that parents will purchase stuff for each other's kids, even though those kids don't need more stuff. Second, it is a way of obtaining said stuff your child does not need so that you might have the common experience of arguing with your kids and saying, "You already have too many toys."

Structurally, the birthday party is a bit more complex, but the steps for attendees are as follows:

* *Find the birthday venue (generally a bouncy, trampoline, or ninja warrior thingy) in a random-a$$ industrial park.*
* *Remark (to yourself), "Hmm, I never knew this place was back here."*
* *Take an awkward walk from car to venue with that one parent whose name you can never remember and whose kid threw pizza at your kid at the last party.*
* *Drop the gift (shoddily thrown together in a gift bag that you assembled in the parking lot) into a large gift-holding receptacle.*
* *Sign the waiver promising that if your kid gets hurt at the venue, you won't sue.*
* *Watch your kid nearly lose a tooth at the venue in celebration of the waiver. See other kid nearly get trampled. Also in celebration of the waiver.*
* *Eat five or six half-slices of lukewarm pizza and wash down with four ounces of lukewarm, diluted lemonade.*
* *Take part in a horribly sung rendition of the Happy Birthday Song.*
* *Eat a slice of sheet cake. Note that the cake was also the only thing your child ate this entire time (important later).*
* *Take your sweaty, sugared-up mess back to the car.*
* *Stop at a fast food joint on the way home. Note that your child seems...a bit on edge.*
* *Prepare for tears when your child realizes: a) he did not receive gifts today and b) the cheap goody bag toy already broke.*
* *Repeat this cycle next Saturday.*

Do me a favor: ask for books for your child. Or ask for a donation to a worthy cause. Your in-laws already bought you enough Legos.

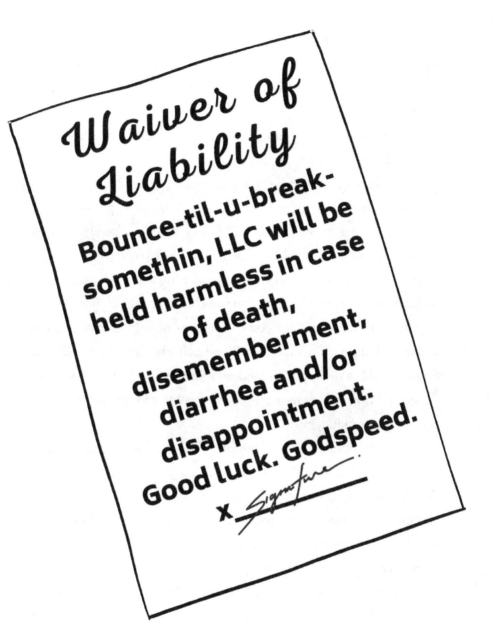

#36. Playground Geopolitics

There is a cold war happening right now at the playground. Let's talk about some sovereign nation-states you may encounter while you're out there traveling.

***FYI. Just in case you had a weak social studies class in middle school, these are not actual places.

The United States of Zero Supervision: Maybe she truly doesn't care about her kids; more likely, she just has a ton going on that makes it difficult to watch her child. You know you've arrived here because you've already asked, "Does this kid have a parent?" They might be running to the car to grab something while Billy picks up a stick and tries to eat it. Maybe they are chasing younger siblings. The important thing here is for you to use your diplomat skills and just adopt the kid for a few minutes while she finishes her phone call. Her four-year-old is definitely as wild as yours, so pitch in and keep an eye out for him. We all have citizenship here from time to time, so do your best not to judge.

Over-Structured-Land: If a mom tells you that she has to leave the playground at 3:57 PM to make it to Karate class by 4:15 PM and then has to pick up her other kid from aftercare at 4:35 PM, this may be a bit high-anxiety to get involved with, and I say *avoid*. The inhabitants here may be nice, but at some point they're going to be hard to keep track of. In Over-Structured-Land, they run the kids ragged and suck out the joy. Hang out, but I wouldn't buy property here. You're not allowed in without fulfilling the stringent requirements anyway, so it works out.

Bully-Ville: See the section on bullying for the real deal, but if you encounter a mom flying the flag from this war-torn land, you need to engage fully. I know none of us likes conflict, but it takes a village, and these moms need to learn to stop the cycle of bullying. Diplomacy will not work; if you see a bully, it's important to ask the inhabitant, "Whose kid is this?" And let her answer for that nonsense.

The Blowout Islands: We've all vacationed here, but to live here full time? Decadent. How does she do it? Does she come straight from the salon every day for pickup? We'll never know, because citizenship to this country requires a secret code few moms can decipher. More power to you, but I couldn't live there; it's too much work to maintain that level of coiffing.

The People's Republic of Gossip and Outlying Territories: This is a very noisy country. The inhabitants here are easy to engage, but at some point it's gonna be too much for you. Just be nice, won't you? Nobody cares that Susan is getting a divorce. Except them. This is an island of despair surrounded by an ocean of trouble. Don't speak their language; mamas gotta take care of each other.

The Commonwealth of Dad: The most isolated little country there is. These guys just show up at the playground, no friends, non-stop screaming kids just driving them nuts. Most of the time they just wave and stay far away. Let them be on their phones and give them an assist every now and then. They're just trying to keep the kids in one piece; however, certain inhabitants may have learned some of the mom code and are considered Cool Dads.

The Isle of Mom: See section on Mom Code and you're in!

#37. HOMEWORK...ALREADY?

Duke professor Harris Cooper coined the "ten-minute rule" for homework. Students should receive ten minutes of homework per day, starting in first grade, and ten additional minutes each subsequent year. By twelfth grade that would mean completing 120 minutes of daily homework. Got it? Cool.

So why the F does my second grader have an hour of homework?

It's complicated.

To some degree, the tail has wagged the dog on this issue. Increasingly educated parents have pushed schools into making grade-school instruction increasingly hard, all while kids are already getting less unstructured play time and outdoor exercise due to a variety of other pressures (video games, smartphones, social media).

So what's a parent to do?

On the one hand, you are at the whim of your school district. If Rachel is getting an hour of homework every night, you can't exactly let her sink. It isn't really feasible to up and relocate. But you can have your voice heard by engaging actively in the parent-teacher organization or by meeting with your child's teacher. Maybe your child needs some extra time, extra help, or specialized assistance that the school can help you navigate.

Children seem to do best in school when they enjoy going to school, not necessarily when they get more intensive schooling. So, ask for help! It's ok. It doesn't mean your kid is bad or that you're bad. It just means school has gotten intense these days, and you need some assistance.

Looking for some academic help? Check out:
* www.ck12.org
* www.quizlet.com
* www.khanacademy.org

#38. Bullies Are Just Little Jerks

Let's face it, kids can be brutal. Some of it is just a raw, unadulterated lack of social graces. Some of it is god-awful parenting whereby kids learn to be sh*theads and keep the cycle of sh*theadedness going forever. Either way, that's your baby out there, and ain't nobody got time for that nonsense.

***BTW, if your kid is a bully, acknowledge that mess and fix it (and fix yourself if you contributed to that behavior).

Don't get me wrong, kids need to learn resilience, and they need to fend for themselves, but you need to face this sort of stuff head-on when it occurs.

It can be hard to tell whether your kid is being bullied, so here are some tips (adapted from stopbullying.gov):

How do I know my child is being bullied?

* Look for changes in their behavior but remember not all kids will show warning signs because they may be embarrassed.

Some signs that may point to bullying:

* Unexplainable injuries
* Lost or destroyed personal items
* Frequent sickness or faking sickness to stay home
* Changes in eating habits, like suddenly skipping meals or binge eating. Kids may come home from school hungry because they did not eat lunch.
* Sleep changes
* Declining grades, loss of interest in schoolwork, or not wanting to go to school

* Sudden loss of friends or avoidance of social situations
* Feelings of helplessness or decreased self-esteem
* Self-destructive behaviors or words
* Signs your kid may be a bully or is more likely to bully:
* Physical or verbal fights
* Having friends who bully others
* Increasingly aggressive behaviors
* Getting frequent detentions at school
* Coming home with unexplained extra money or new belongings
* Blaming others for their problems or actions
* Overly competitive, worrying about their reputation or popularity

Why didn't my kid tell me?

Statistics show that an adult was notified in less than half (40 percent) of bullying incidents. Kids don't tell adults for many reasons:

* Bullying can make a child feel helpless. Kids may want to handle it on their own to feel in control again. They may fear being seen as weak or a tattletale.
* Kids may fear backlash from the kid who bullied them.
* Bullying can be a humiliating experience. Kids may not want adults to know what is being said about them, whether true or false. They may also fear that adults will judge them or punish them for being weak.
* Kids who are bullied may already feel socially isolated. They may feel like no one cares or could understand.

* Kids may fear being rejected by their peers. Friends can help protect kids from bullying, and kids can fear losing this support.

While much of the information here is important, there are some intangibles worth considering as well. For one, consider the sort of behavior (from other kids) you will tolerate. In preschool, our son encountered a bully (surprising for such young kids). This kid had an older brother and was much more mature in his ability to be a rotten jerk than your average, sweet four-year-old. He was exclusionary, encouraged other kids to gang up on our son, and left him in tears many times. Throughout this ordeal, my husband and I had similar feelings about what we should do, but our thresholds for blowing it up were different. The last thing you want during a rough patch for your kid is internal strife as a couple or a single parent. We were able to help our son get through this nonsense because we got on the same page, and fast. The next step was working with the school and ultimately, everything worked out.

As kids get older, it's important to realize that you can't, nor should you, solve all their problems. This creates a fine line for you as a mama. So, the overarching thing to keep in mind is creating an environment at home where they can tell you anything at any time. Sure, kids are more resilient than we think, and the fact is, they are likely solving problems at school without you knowing it. But, when things spill over, you have to start asking questions. We've all seen way too many stories of kids being cyber-bullied to the point of suicide. Protecting them from bullying can be a life-saver.

If your child is being bullied, here are some resources that may help:

www.stopbullying.gov is a great resource for all things bullying, including mental health counseling, resources available for parents and kids, and helpful tips and tricks.

If serious bodily injury is known or suspected, call 911.

If your child is expressing suicidal or dangerous thoughts, contact the National Suicide Prevention Lifeline (online or at 1-800-273-TALK).

#39. TEN RULES FOR A SUCCESSFUL PLAYDATE

Playdates are the life's blood of the mama and child social equation. For moms, this is their chance to hang out with another adult human. For children, this is their chance to become socialized and have fun. By the time both of these things become true, your child will be old enough to not want you to refer to these meet-ups as playdates, but that's life.

The ten rules are:
1. Feverishly clean the house
   (only to have it destroyed in minutes)
2. Hide the laundry pile
   (someone may get lost in it)
3. Go to Whole Foods for organic snacks
   (because appearances)
4. Get the coffee maker ready
   (you're going to need it)
5. Find out about food allergies and other important considerations

(also make sure you let the host know about these when you're the guest)

6. Hide your kid's favorite toys

(the other kids will find and break the best stuff)

7. Set a time limit

(two hours is a good place to start with little ones until they prove they can hold it together)

8. Prepare to be interrupted

(your conversations will be cut into snippets, so get ready)

9. Be kind to each other's children

(on any given day, your kid is gonna be the jerk, have empathy)

10. Wind the playdate down with some television

(an hour of intense play can really wipe them out and make them squirrelly; it's ok to just veg at the end)

#40. OVERSCHEDULED KIDS: I DON'T WANT TO WAKE UP EARLY ON SATURDAY, EITHER

The odds of a high school football player becoming an NFL superstar are, let's just say, not encouraging. Sure, youth sports keep your kids fit and teach them sportsmanship. But the chances that little Lucy becomes the next Serena Williams are slight.

The same is true of the many academic enrichment classes available these days. Sure it's great that your four-year-old can name all the presidents, but parlor tricks have captured our imagination for years and have yet to yield the innovators or thought leaders; maybe a few Jeopardy contestants have been developed, though.

Now, I'm not knocking your kids if they play five sports or are exceedingly bright. Far from it. What I am cautioning you about is the sport of parenting. In a modern, performance-driven world, busyness is currency. "I'm running to cheerleading, then we have karate, then we have swimming, then we'll eat dinner in the car on our way to drum lessons." Many of our schedules have become an endless to-do list. And for what? And to what end? Just make sure you aren't laying expectations on your kid for no appreciable benefit.

In his book, *The Over-Scheduled Child*, Alvin Rosenfeld, MD, contends that parents in a pursuit of parenting triumph are micromanaging their children's schedules at the expense of their entire family's well-being. He details how some of these children reach their teenage years burned out and no longer interested in participation in their once-beloved activities. Most of these kids are, in a sense, set up to fail when they realize they won't be making it to the NFL.

I get it. Many parents are thinking that Little League games are their kid's ticket to Stanford. Or that they played the violin, so their kids need to learn an instrument now, too. But according to Dr. Rosenfeld (and many experts in the field), this sort of mentality may lead to worsening anxiety, sleep patterns, and depression in childhood. In childhood!

I'm *all* for activities that spark joy in our children and are a good fit for the family. Some research suggests that being heavily scheduled with extracurricular activities isn't necessarily a bad thing, *for the right kid*. Kids need some structure and being part of a team or throwing themselves into hobbies are useful pursuits. But you have to ask yourself: why are we doing this? Are we building that resume for a budding captain of industry by making Junior cry after they lost a game? Are we training the next Michael Phelps by pushing her to exhaustion? Are we projecting our own desires, failures, or hang-ups on our babies?

The key word is *balance*. Most educators and researchers agree there's no optimal number of activities; it depends on the kid. Even those who advocate for multiple activities still encourage parents to make time for their children to just be bored and to let them figure out how to fill their time. Doing nothing can itself be an activity (it shouldn't be their only activity); the ability to turn downtime into something fun and meaningful and creative is a true gift. This will serve your kids well into young adulthood when boredom/disappointment/loneliness can be turned into self-destructive behavior. That's a gift more important than being able to catch a fly ball.

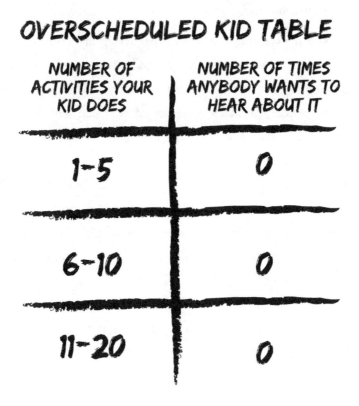

OVERSCHEDULED KID TABLE

NUMBER OF ACTIVITIES YOUR KID DOES	NUMBER OF TIMES ANYBODY WANTS TO HEAR ABOUT IT
1-5	0
6-10	0
11-20	0

Want to learn more about encouraging independent play? Check out:

https://letgrow.org for strategies, games, and resources about fostering children's independence and confidence.

#41. What is a Yeet?: Are We Speaking the Same Lingo?

Kid: "Yeet!"

Me: "Are you swearing at me?"

Kid: "Totes not. Periodt.

Me: "Huh? I don't understand."

Kid: "WhY aRe YoU YeLLInG aT mE?"

Me: "I am completely lost."

If this conversation sounds familiar, congratulations! You may have a teenager or a tween on your hands. Every youth culture has slang proprietary to them, like "rad," "totally," or "as if!" What sets this current generation apart is the speed at which new words catch on. When California valley girls said, "gag me with a spoon" in the '80s, it took movies and television shows for it to catch on outside of California. Then in the '90s, anything Cher Horowitz said in *Clueless* became the latest slang. Now with social media, both spoken language and typed terms spread at the speed of light. Just as you feel comfortable saying, "siiiiiick" to describe a good thing, then there's a new word like "gucci" to replace it. Gucci?

This makes me feel like I'm one hundred years old, but here it goes: when I don't know a new phrase, I go straight to Urbandictionary. com to look it up. There are also a few phone apps that can help you translate teen slang, such as SlangIt: The Slang Dictionary and the

Chat Slang Dictionary. They can help you decode your teen's speech, particularly if they are speaking in code about possibly dangerous behavior. Don't get all nosy, just make sure it's safe, totally obnoxious slang. It's gucci…until it isn't. Periodt (yes, I realize there is a "T" at the end of the word "period," apparently that's a thing now).

#42. Ha! You Don't Understand Math Anymore

Let's just talk about my least favorite of all subjects, Mathematics. I'll admit, this was the area where I was always weakest. I got out of undergrad alive, but mostly because math was an ornamental skill for a firmly Liberal Arts major like me; however, I do consider my ability to do third grade math pretty strong. At least I did, until my first-grader brought home this math problem:

COMMON CORE MATH

$$295$$
$$+68$$
$$\overline{363}$$ Wrong!

Correct!

After drawing lines and dots and circling things and shading in some blobs, a wave of panic swept me thinking, "We're only talking about first grade math! It's math! Didn't we send mathematical proofs into space in the 1970s thinking it was the universal language? What happened with that?" It's fine. I've hired a math tutor, and my classes start tomorrow!

Seriously, if you need some help, I highly recommend the following resources so you can re-learn/un-learn math and help your kids:

Common Core Math for Parents for Dummies by Christopher Danielson. Yes, they wrote a book for us; that's how bad this stuff is.

Also, check out:

http://www.corestandards.org/Math/ All the stuff your kids will be learning, by grade level.

#43. ADVOCATE FOR YOUR KID! THE CHILD WITH SPECIAL NEEDS

Special needs is a very broad term, meant to cover a wide variety of diagnoses and conditions, from those that resolve quickly to those that will be lifelong, from mild to severe.

This is not a medical book. This is not even a child development book. This book is about empowering mamas, sharing some tips, and having a few laughs. But the designation of special needs is important to consider, and covers a *lot* of our kids, so we need to talk.

Whether your child has medical, behavioral, developmental, learning, or mental health challenges, there has never been a better time to advocate for your child. Run, don't walk toward assistance.

If you think something is up, talk about it with your partner, with a teacher, with your pediatrician. And don't go against your instinct or let denial get in the way. Trust your gut. If you think something is up, it probably is. If it isn't, then good, now you know. Advocate for your kid so they don't suffer, miss out, or get left behind. You won't forgive yourself if they do.

From an increasing acceptance of mental health issues to improved diagnosis and therapy for conditions such as autism, moms are seeking help for their kids more than ever. This is a good thing. It is not a sign that things are getting worse! It does not mean our kids are weaker than kids were years ago. The stigma attached to many of these special challenges has lessened, and the time is now. Advocate for your child!

Learn more about advocating for your child:
* www.understood.org - Understood for All is an organization offering helpful resources for individuals with diverse thinking.
* www.childmind.org - The Child Mind Institute provides valuable information for children and families struggling with mental health and learning disorders.
* www.ncld.org - National Center for Learning Disabilities empowers parents through education.
* www.autismspeaks.org - Autism Speaks provides advocacy and support for families with children on the spectrum.

#44. SILENCE IS NOT AN OPTION: ALLYSHIP

With national protests against racial inequality and a growing awareness of issues facing folks in the LGBTQ community, the need for allyship across the board has become more apparent than ever. It's not enough to not be racist or prejudiced against people not fitting a certain mold. It is a parent's responsibility to teach their children to be anti-racist and tolerant of differences. We can achieve this through education and allyship. No mother birthed her children thinking, "I'm gonna raise a racist, sexist little a-hole." But yet, these people still exist all around us.

With some guidance from Guidetoallyship.com, to be an ally is to:

*   Take on a struggle as your own.
*   Translate the benefits of your privilege (whatever it may be) to those who lack it.
*   Amplify voices of the oppressed.
*   Acknowledge that even though you feel pain, the conversation is not always about you.
*   Stand up, even when you feel scared.
*   Own your mistakes (and don't be afraid to make them).
*   Understand that your education is up to you and no one else.

In addition to actively working toward allyship, it's important to remember that kindness starts at home. In my son's elementary school, the administration focuses its curriculum on five key points, I.C.A.R.E. Everything that happens within the walls of the school is related to I.C.A.R.E. I'm sharing it here because it has been a wonderful part of my son's education and development into a kind boy. Pass it on!

I.C.A.R.E. is about:

*   Integrity: Being honest in your thoughts and actions.
*   Caring: Being compassionate and polite.
*   Attitude: Maintaining a positive attitude.

* Respect: Treating others with consideration and kindness.
* Empathy: Trying to feel what others would be feeling.

Because I.C.A.R.E. has five words, the symbol for it is a hand with each finger representing a word. When I want to remind my son to act with I.C.A.R.E., I can hold up my hand as a prompt. So every time you see a hand held up, you can think I.C.A.R.E. If every parent can teach their children I.C.A.R.E., the next generation will be an unstoppable force for equality. High five for that!

Here's a book list for reading with your children (and yourself):
* Check out the #1000BlackGirlBooks list assembled by Marley Dias (with one thousand books to choose from, you're bound to find something your children like!)
* *A Kids Book About Racism* by Jelani Memory
* *A Kids Book About Empathy* by Daron K. Roberts
* *UnSelfie: Why Empathetic Kids Succeed in Our All-About-Me World* by Michele Borba

#45. Harvard Is on the Phone: School Readiness Prep

"Did you know that So-and-so is reading already?"

"Did you hear she did school prep classes all summer, and they're considering putting her in first grade already?"

"If we can get into this preschool, it's a real steppingstone to Harvard."

From the earliest moments, modern parents feel the pressure to buy products to give their children the educational "edge." Remember *Baby Einstein*? I knew parents who plugged their babies into hours upon hours of those videos because they bought into the hype. Ironically, The American Academy of Pediatrics discourages media use for kids younger than eighteen to twenty-four months. Instead of playing *Baby Einstein* videos, they say parents should kick it old school when it comes to promoting brain development; concentrate on proven methods such as talking, playing, singing, smiling, and reading with your children.

For toddlers and young school-age children, there are one-million-and-one educational games, toys, and apps. Most of them are bright, colorful, and useful for teaching basic skills such as counting, shapes, or letters. A well-meaning parent may let her child play the games *ad nauseam* because, "Oh, it's educational, and it's going to help him get ahead in school."

All I can say is, don't get trapped in this cycle or let it add to your mom guilt. These products play into a very modern fear that your child will not become successful simply because you did not enroll them in chess at age five. Don't fool yourself into thinking that because the name Einstein is in the title of *Little Einsteins* or *Baby Einstein*, that your kid will become the next Einstein. Maybe lower those expectations again.

Don't get me wrong. Education is incredibly important for the overall well-being and outcome of one's life. And there is probably no better way to improve socioeconomic status; however, please don't think that watching videos or playing iPad games are a replacement for human interaction and play.

Maria Montessori said it best: *Play* is the work of the child.

Ok, Pop Quiz Time...

Question: Harvard receives roughly 40,000 applications a year and admits roughly 2,000 new students each year. If the number of applicants who listened to Baby Einstein *increased by 50 percent next year, how many more students would Harvard accept (circle the correct answer)?*

0,   10,   500,   1,000

Answer: 0

#46. "It's Gonna Blow!": Triumph over Tantrums

Tantrums can turn a day on its head. Or an entire year on its head. One minute you're finishing a cup of coffee, and the next minute your sweet cherub morphs into a hot lava monster. I sat down with Dr. Matthew Goldfine, PhD, a clinical psychologist, for guidance on how to triumph over tantrums.

Me: Dr. Matt, please help us modern moms!

Dr. Matt: Sure!

* Tantrums happen to everyone.

  Consider this part of being a parent. Just like how some days the weather is bad or your favorite TV show has a crummy episode. Accept this as part of the job and don't take it personally.

* Take emotion out of the equation.

  If your child's tantrum is a pot of boiling water, do you want your emotions to be the fire keeping it hot or the ice cubes that cool it down? Be emotionally neutral and calm so you don't make a bad tantrum even worse. Don't allow yourself to be provoked.

* Sometimes, the best thing to do is walk away.

  Your attention (even negative attention) can fuel a tantrum. What you say, how you say it, and even your facial expressions can make a tantrum go from bad to worse. If you can't be a silent, calm observer, it is better to get some distance and walk away. In other words, ignoring a tantrum is fundamental to it ending.

* The bigger they are, the harder they fall (...or the louder the tantrum, the faster it fizzles).

Dealing with a loud, emotional, intense tantrum? That usually means your child will tire themselves out. Don't get suckered into engaging with them and just let their intense energy run its course. Often in a few minutes, they are starting to cool down.

* Be more stubborn than your child.

You must, must, must hold firm. If you issue a consequence, then you make it your business to always follow through. If you promise a reward, then the same rules apply. If you tell your child that there is no dessert until they finish their vegetables, then no matter how much they kick and scream, there is no ice cream until their broccoli is eaten. Kids quickly learn the difference between a parent who doesn't follow through and one whose word is set in stone.

* Be consistent.

I joke with my patients that I would rather they do the wrong thing consistently than the right thing inconsistently. Reacting in a predictable way every time there is a tantrum (e.g., the words you use, your reaction, and your behavior) means that your child will eventually start to minimize tantrums before they even take place. After all, if they already know what the outcome will be, why bother going through with a tantrum?

* Try faking a conversation.

One of the tricks of the trade that I offer parents is during a tantrum (when we are ignoring and not speaking to the child), you can utilize a fake conversation with your partner or phone call that can give the child a helpful piece of information. Imagine something like, "Hi, Aunt Suzie… yes, Connor is having a tough time…of course, whenever he calms down and puts his shoes away, he can go back to drawing his picture…all he has to do is use his quiet voice for ten seconds and I will come back into the room…" I have found that beyond being a reminder for your child, it serves as a nice distraction, which can break the tantrum cycle.

* Always try to look to the positive.

Even though there is an instinct to fight fire with fire and address a tantrum with your own yelling and threats (AKA an adult tantrum), finding a way to praise desirable behavior is a far more sustainable and effective way of preventing tantrums from occurring in the first place. Even after a tantrum occurs, look for something to praise. Did your child calm down quickly? Did your child clean up the mess that was made without you asking? No matter how intense a tantrum is, it will eventually end, which gives you an opportunity to praise the behavior that you want to see in the first place.

Me: Thank you for your advice, Dr. Matt!

#47. Nerf Guns Should Come with a Free Pair of Goggles

No matter your stance on gun control, these toys will make it into your house. My husband and I had a pretty firm stance on guns as toys until our son was roughly six. That was the year we were invited to our first Nerf gun birthday party, and it was also the year he got a very nice semi-automatic foam cannon from one of his uncles.

We tried to avoid the Nerf train but it found us, like a heat-seeking, mass-produced destroyer of vases. And I have to admit, having a Nerf gun fight is actually a ton of fun. So here is some judgment-free info about Nerf guns.

1. Your child might say, "It's Nerf or nuffin" a thousand times before you understand that marketing really is a wonder to behold.

2. The smaller pistols seem to actually shoot harder and hurt more than the big clunky ones they can barely hold up and load. Spend the extra ten dollars if it is in your budget.

3. It doesn't matter how soft something feels when it's stationary. Sure, those bullets are made of foam. But when they become projectiles, they can inflict some serious damage and pain. From what I can gather from research, the average blaster fires these foam darts at around seventy feet per second! Eye protection is a minimum requirement, and you need to cover up any exposed skin as much as possible.

4. You can often distract from becoming a target yourself by making a proper target for them to hit. Take a Target bag (I know you have many), tape it to a pillow, and you have a safe living room until that gets boring and they start shooting you again.

5. Clear the tables of anything you value. Not only will they become collateral damage, but kids do not seem to believe that glass shards are sharp or dangerous and will be attracted to the shiny mess they have created.

6. Research studies have shown that there is no link between young children playing with toy guns and later aggression and violence. In fact, psychologists say symbolic play, understanding good and evil, may actually be healthy. So take a breath, they're going to be fine. Your picture frames on the other hand....

#48. THE IMPORTANCE OF TEACHING YOUR KIDS ABOUT "GOOD MUSIC"

We're not going to talk about what constitutes good music here, so don't get excited. That is your prerogative, and I can't tell you what to listen to. But one area where you can actually exert positive control over your kid's development is by preventing them from becoming a person with zero taste in music. You know the ones.

Put your foot down early. Sure, they are going to listen to the Wheels on the Bus and all the standard kid music, but did we make sure our son fell asleep to Bob Marley every night for the first nine months of his life? Pretty much. Did we sing those songs to him as we rocked him to sleep every night? You know it. Has he been to birthday parties with a poor, sad guitar guy who is asking for requests from the kids when my son calls out, "Play Guns N Roses!"? You're damned right.

Look, it's great to expose your child to lots of different kinds of music, and you should. But do you want to be cooler than your sixteen-year-old one day? I think not. Play some great music, and play it all the time. Play the songs that mean something to you. Maybe find a censored version of the first Wu-Tang Clan album and bob your heads in the car. Maybe convince your kid that this AC/DC song is actually entitled "Highway to HELP" (worked for us). Sing Queen's "You're My Best Friend" to them over and over again. But don't think that because they're little people they need to listen to "Baby Shark" on repeat.

Everybody loses in that scenario.

#49. Fluffy Balls of Responsibility: Kids Want Pets

You'll hear it all the time. We're not dog people. We're not cat people. We're not animal people. Well, you better go down to Richard's Wonderful World of Reptiles and become an animal person, because your kid wants a pet. Already have a pet, you say? Doesn't matter. They want another pet, not some old pet that predates their arrival on the planet. We've had most of the available iterations of pet in our house, so here's a rundown for your consideration.

Fish: Relaxing, right? No, that means boring. Carnival goldfish are already circling the drain, but they serve as a gateway drug. You will win a goldfish. You will feel like an awesome parent. You will get it home and buy a ton of stuff to house this sad creature. It will die within three days. Your child will cry. You will go to the pet shop and get another fish. Your child won't care about these fish, though, so you will care for them, replace them as they, too, go to fishy heaven, and pretty soon nobody will care. Those are your fish, so if *you* want a fish, get your kid a fish.

Reptiles/frogs: These things are cool, plain and simple. Snakes, lizards, frogs. They look cool. They do cool stuff. They even eat frozen mice and crickets and stuff. But unless you grew up on a lizard farm, the major barrier to entry here is gonna be cleaning their cages.

They're great pets, just sitting under their heat lamps, and then you realize you have to reach in there and grab…a snake? I did not sign up for grabbing snakes or lizards. Also, some of them eat live crickets. Which is cool, but did you know crickets make noise all night long? It sounds kind of quaint when you go for an evening stroll, but not so much when they're in the house. Then they're just a wrecker of sleep.

Small rodents: Gerbils, hamsters, and ferrets. Cute and cuddly, no doubt. I had a gerbil as a kid. It had babies. Awwwww. It ate all the babies and tore them apart like gummy bears. You do what you will with that information. Proceed with caution.

Cats: Otherwise known as Not-Dogs, cats are the maligned domestic animal of the century. Sure, they secretly judge you. Sure, they can come in brands ranging from snippy to openly hostile. But, the right cat can be a great pet. Don't buy this whole, my-cat-is-like-a-dog thing, though. If you want it to love you and give you unconditional acceptance, you are setting yourself up for disappointment. Still, kittens are really the best and cutest little things, and unlike dogs, they know how to not poop all over your house.

Dogs: Ahhhh, man's best friend. Nothing loves you like a dog. For a classic childhood pet experience, there is no greater animal. With you everywhere you go. Happy to see you when you come home. Sad when you're sad. A dog is a part of your life that will be almost all positive. Except it's an infant that never grows up and a bull in the china closet for the entirety of its life. Did you clean the baseboard in your house in the past? Don't bother now, it'll only remind you how scratched it all is. Did you used to love sweet smells in the family room? Don't bother, the whole couch smells like wet dog farts. Sorry, dogs are great, but they will dominate you real fast. You better be ready. They also eat baby bottles and chickie nuggies without fail.

PET DECISION GRID

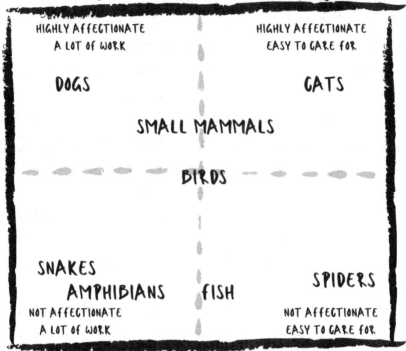

Tarantulas/hissing cockroaches and other weird things: Pass. Hard pass.

#50. KIDS GET TIRED OF MOMMY SOMETIMES: AN ODE TO GRANDPARENTS

If you are fortunate enough to have your parents in your life, congratulations, your kid has grandparents.

Ah, I have such fond memories of my grandparents. But didn't your mom always seem a little miffed at your grandparents when you were a kid? Why was that?

I get it now....

Want to stick to a certain bedtime routine? Nah.

A strict "no cookies for breakfast" rule? Have fun, the kid's gotta eat!

General avoidance of power tools? Oh, he's got it under control.

Here's what you need to appreciate about grandparents. They have their own rules. And what I have learned is that's actually ok. In fact, that's part of the fun. Sure you're gonna pick up the sugar monster who may or may not have slept four hours last night. Sure, your kid is going to say that grandma's pasta with butter recipe is far superior to yours. But when you ask them if they had a nice time at grandma's, they're gonna say *yes*. And as a kid, it's great to know how loved you are and to learn from grandparents, who might as well be from another planet as far as kids are concerned.

Our kids get a lot of sh*t everywhere they go. They really do. We're all over them for schoolwork, behavior, screen time, manners, you name it. Going to their grandparents' house is like an all-inclusive stay at the Ritz. Where else could a kid go and wash down donuts with an ice pop? Grandparents are the best!

#51. Listening to Your Kids: An Interview with a Real Kid

This guidebook is written by a parent for parents. But I wanted to write a chapter on listening to our children. Too often we look at our kids as passive vessels that need filling. In reality, they have a ton to say, and sometimes all I need to do is listen to my son to solve many of the challenges we face together.

Listening is a critical parenting skill. So now it's my turn to take a backseat on this journey and let my child navigate for a bit. I asked him for some parenting advice and this is some of what he said.

Me: I want some parenting advice, ok? What advice would you give mommies in order for them to be good mommies?

My son: Since I'm a kid, I know a lot about moms. Trust me with what I'm about to say.

Me: (Dying from cuteness overload from his intro)

My son: Moms need to be *nice* to their kids.

Kids don't like being bossed around. Some kids like to be independent to show off for their moms. And we can do lots of stuff, you know.

When a kid is sad, his parents should give him a hug or a compliment or just say something nice. If the kids run to their bedrooms, don't chase them. They may want alone time. Give them space for a little bit. I personally like alone time when I want it, and I can come back when I am ready.

Oh, and moms should pay attention to their kids. Kids say, "Look at me! Pay attention to me." Look at them because it's hard to hold a handstand, and they may never be able to do it ever again the same way. Pay attention because kids are doing amazing things! You might miss them.

Kids like snacks. Give them a few snacks a day, especially mid-day in between the main food times. That's when snacks taste the best.

Kids don't like to be rushed. When parents rush them, it may make the kids confused or annoyed. It takes me time to do things like get ready to leave or to eat.

Kids need lots of playtime. Lots of it. It's literally a kid's favorite thing to do! Playtime. Lots of it. Can't say it enough.

Kids like sweet things, like ice pops and candy.

Kids like homework to be fun. Make our work more fun and it goes faster.

Kids like their birthdays. Try to celebrate it for a season, a month, or a week. Not a year, because it can't be your birthday every day. But for me, I like a week. Or a month even.

Kids like to have company over that won't steal toys or break things or make a big poop anywhere in the house.

Kids like pets. Cats, dogs, birds, and fish make good pets. Don't get anything that will hurt the kids when they play with them. Like a cobra. Cobras are also expensive.

If the kids are having fun in the bath, extend their time because they like to play. It makes up for any cuts in playtime with longer playing in the bath.

Kids love to snuggle, especially with moms because moms are soft and warm.

Some kids are shy and that's ok. Don't ask these kids too many questions. One or two are ok. Don't bomb kids with questions because it makes them feel shyer.

Try to make everything fun with kids. Kids want to have fun unless they feel sad (then leave them alone until they are ready to talk, like I said before).

Don't scream at kids. It scares and confuses them. If it happens a lot, it will make kids wish they had different parents. I know because I have friends like that. They get scared of their parents.

Kids like to play outside. But if a kid is in the mood to stay inside, let him.

Me: That's great, buddy. Thanks for all the information. Is there anything you want to say to sum it all up?

My son: Kids like to have their opinions heard. They have important things to say. Moms should listen.

Before you were a mom, you were someone. That someone still matters.

Chapter 5

YOU PROBS

efore you were their mother, you were someone. This chapter celebrates *you*, the twenty-first century mother. You're still you, only now you got some kids. Remember that!

#52. SELF-CARE: THE MOST OVERUSED WORD OF THE MILLENNIUM

"Oh, just get your nails done."

"Have a spa day then you'll feel better."

"A bath will rejuvenate your spirit."

"Scream into a pillow, then you can deal with your family again."

Ok, maybe the last one actually works (my husband taught me that one, seriously).

Self-care, the most overused word of the millennium, provides us the hope of refreshing and recharging our batteries. There are hundreds of books about self-care. Brands are dedicated to it. It's becoming a trope, but that doesn't make it any less important.

Yes, we know we need to take care of ourselves. Yes, trust me, we want to. No one *wants* to feel like they are running on empty. But self-care is a matter of how and when, and how feasible is it? As mothers, we pour so much from our bucket that we often have mere droplets left at the end of the day. Self-care is more than just upkeeping your aesthetics, like nails or roots (if those are important to you, then rock on, girl!).

For me, self-care has been about identifying what depletes me—persons, places, things. If this resonates with you, I suggest you write it out in a journal. Bullet point it. See it. Cross it out. And then take some action by avoiding these energy vampires to change your situation. Toxic relationships with friends and family members can suck your battery faster than your kid playing video games on your cell phone while Mom keeps calling you about something.

Self-care is actually self-preservation. Saying "no" to people's constant demands of you may be your form of self-care. Telling your significant other you need a few minutes of uninterrupted quiet to be yours. Don't diminish it, whatever it is. It's just as important as taking an hour to fill in your acrylics or blow out your hair.

Things that Recharge My Batteries:

5.) Taking a shower *and* shaving my legs

4.) When my husband makes me coffee without my asking

3.) When my son lets me use the bathroom and scroll in peace

2.) Sitting in the car in my driveway to finish listening to that song I haven't heard in years

1.) A playdate with a mom who "gets it" and totally restores my faith in humanity

Since I know how to charge *my* batteries, I wanted to speak with an expert about recharging *your* batteries, so I asked Dr. Jennifer Blossom, occupational therapist, CEO/founder of *Blossoming Moms* to share her secrets.

Here are Dr. Blossom's top five tips to simplify your motherhood:

1. Define your priorities.

   If schedules, responsibilities, and the commitments of your day-to-day life make motherhood feel more like a big blur instead of a meaningful journey, then you need to start prioritizing, girl! Begin prioritizing by listing out the top three things that are most important to you and your family. From there, be okay with saying "no" to everything else. This habit will help you intentionally build a life focused on what matters most, instead of filling your days with the busy demands of the world around you.

2. Create pockets of rest throughout your days.

   Just like your phone needs to recharge its low battery, so do you, Mama! You can't expect to live as the best version of yourself when your battery is running low, right? This is why intentionally creating pockets of time throughout your day to refocus, recenter, and recharge is so important.

   These intentional pockets of time can be as long or as short as your schedule allows and should allow you to relax your brain and your body.

   Ideas to get you started: go for a walk, drink a smoothie, bask in the sunshine (technology free!), listen to calming music, plug into an inspiring podcast.

3. Create a simple, daily smoothie routine.

   Drinking a daily smoothie is a simple, healthy habit that not only skyrockets your energy, but will also give you an extra boost of nutrition—a double win for keeping up with those kiddos. Plus, smoothies are both time and budget friendly making it a #winwin for the entire family.

PRO MOM TIP: Prep your smoothie the night before by portioning out fruits and veggies. Voilà! Blend your smoothie first thing in the morning for a refreshing and powerful start to your day.

Dr. Blossom's Favorite Smoothie Recipe:

Pineapple Mango Smoothie Bowl:

Serving size 1

Ingredients:

1 cup frozen mango

½ cup frozen pineapple

½ banana

¼ cup chopped cauliflower

1 cup spinach

1¼ cup almond milk or non-dairy milk of choice (thicker add more, thinner less)

1 tsp chia seed

1 tsp flaxseed

1 scoop of protein powder *optional

Directions:

Place all ingredients into a high-powered blender.

Pulse for ten seconds, then blend on high for one minute or until well blended. Pour into your favorite glass and enjoy!

4. Master your meal planning.

   Simplify your meal planning process by taking one hour over the weekend to plan your meals for the upcoming week. Start by planning out your family's dinners, then keep a simple rotation of healthy breakfasts, lunches, and snacks to switch up throughout the week. It does take a little extra time and effort to meal plan, but it will save you *so* much stress, time, and money in the long run.

   PRO MOM TIP: After you've planned your meals for the week, plan a "once a week" grocery store run. Aiming to go to the store just once a week instead of multiple times throughout the week will also help save you time and money.

5. Develop a cleaning routine.

   Keeping up with housework can oftentimes feel like a job in itself (*Newsflash…It totally is!*), which is why having a flexible, simple cleaning routine is so important! Instead of spending your entire weekend folding laundry and scrubbing toilets, try creating a daily twenty- to thirty-minute cleaning routine. This routine will help you stay ahead of your house, instead of letting the house duties get the best of you.

   Daily Cleaning Routine:
   - Complete one load of laundry (wash, dry, fold, and put away)
   - Load/unload the dishwasher (start your dishwasher at night and unload it while you're drinking coffee in the morning!)
   - Complete one house chore per day (i.e. floors, bathrooms, windows, etc.).

You can do this, Mama! A simpler approach to motherhood will allow you to create the meaningful motherhood you deserve. Just remember: one thought, one habit, one day at a time.

#53. HYGIENE. STILL A THING. COULDA FOOLED ME!

When my son was a baby, I often lost track of time (hours, days, weeks) because what is time when your schedule revolves around nursing, wiping butts, cooking dinner, folding laundry, bath time, bedtime, waking up at 2:00 AM, rinsing and repeating? Somewhere in that schedule, "Mom's shower" gets lost. It got so bad for me at one point that I would have to write myself a post-it note as a reminder to *take a shower*. Who knows how many days passed since I washed my hair? It seemed permanently stuck in the mom bun position even after I removed the hair tie.

My secret to looking put together when leaving the house to run errands was wearing workout clothes. It's amazing how workout clothes can cover up the fact that you haven't showered in three days and make you look like you have your life together. Of course, saying three days is hyperbolic. It was never that long! Was it?

In the same boat? This section is designed to help you along the continuum of mom hygiene. You don't want to show up to your friend's baby shower smelling like sour milk, do ya? Answer the following questions, add up the points, and see where you're at.

Question 1: Do you smell like...

a. Baby formula, sour milk, diapers, Desitin, or straight-up body odor? 1 point

b. Gamey socks, dirty sweaty hair, maybe some BO? 2 points

c. Nothing, really. Cleanish. 3 points

d. A walking spa from head to toe. 5 points

Question 2: Your face…

a. Looks like it's been through some stuff? 1 point

b. Has bags upon bags under the eyes, some sort of dried stuff anywhere? 2 points

c. Appears clean and toned, like you definitely washed it today, and maybe some mascara thrown in? 3 points

d. Is not only clean, but has more than one item of makeup on it (if not a makeup wearer, does your face look vibrant overall)? 5 points

Question 3: Is your hair…

a. Knotted, tossed around, and not something a stranger should smell? 1 point

b. Messy, but tied back-ish? 2 points

c. Messy, tied back but also with the addition of dry shampoo? 3 points

d. Washed, dried, and down or up in your ideal style? 5 points

Hygiene Ratings:

3–5 points: Tyrannosaurus Mess. The only place you should stick to today is going back to the baby's room for feedings and changings. When you get a chance, hand the baby over to Daddy and take a shower, honey. Or strap them into the bouncy chair and bring them into the bathroom with you.

6–8 points: Pretty Pigpen. You're definitely in there somewhere but you may have lost track of the shower door key a few days ago. You can run an errand or two, clearly the kids need some Pedialyte or something.

9–14 points: Quintessential Queen. The kids have been sleeping through the night so you got your shower on, girl! Yes! Enjoy it. You are radiant inside and out.

15 points: Unicorn. Really?! A 15?! Amazing! Shine on! Teach us your magical ways.

#54. Never Did I Ever Think I'd Do That

We all start out thinking we're going to be one kind of mom. We all end up a little bit different. Or maybe even a lot different. Here are some "never did I ever" topics that have made me ask…Who am I? What sort of parents are we? Who does this sort of stuff?

Enjoy. And don't be so hard on yourself; we're all made into hypocrites at one point or another...

* Used fruit snacks as currency/bribery
* Allowed way too much screen time at restaurants
* Had bedtime inconsistency so great even the kids started to wonder about it
* Fed the fam fast food two times in a day
* Lied about the batteries being empty on that annoying robot toy
* Played the Frozen soundtrack on repeat to get some relative peace
* Cooked separate meals for the adults and kids
* Laughed at potty talk (still always funny)
* Turned on those unboxing videos
* Carried my kid for what felt like miles because he refused to walk
* Held my phone in front of a crying toddler's face to soothe him
* Bought a toy every time we went to the drug store so we could get out of there
* Hid in the bathroom and let my husband handle a tantrum
* Served donuts for breakfast and for dessert later in the day
* Lived on instant pancakes
* Created elaborate bedtime rituals that we knew would only work for a week
* Caught airborne pee before it got all over the floor
* Said my kid was under the weather to get out of a social engagement
* Said my kid was two years younger than his actual age to get a discount
* Skipped pages of books at bedtime

* Got super nervous before a parent-teacher conference that turned out fine
* Covered for the tooth fairy when she failed to show up
* Had to pause to remember when my kid's birthday was
* Lost my temper with my kid and yelled when I should have just walked away

If you've ever done any of the above, congratulations! You are human! Be flexible and be gentle with yourself. You're going to think you will *never* do some of this stuff, and then, welp, there you are.

#55. THE MOM UNIFORM

Mark Zuckerberg

Former President Barack Obama

Steve Jobs

Angelina Jolie

Albert Einstein

Kelly Cutrone

You

What do all of these people have in common? Aside from being extraordinary?! They all wear (or wore) the same thing every day. Powerhouses leading complex, busy lives often check one thing off their endless decision list—what they wear each day. Moms are no different. We may have a closet full of clothes and wear the same four things every day. We have enough on our plates without having to worry about getting dressed up like our pre-kid selves (unless we're really feeling it. And when you're feeling it, then by all means, get it, girl! I'm right there with you!).

So what does this modern mom uniform look like?

* Yoga pants. Because parenting is a full-contact sport (usually black to cover any kid-related stuff thrown your way). Also, when I wear yoga pants I look like I have my life together.

* T-shirt (short sleeve in summer, long sleeve in winter). The softer, the better for cuddles.

* Sneakers or slip-on sneakers. Because moms are always on the run.

* Hat (optional). Especially on "bad dirty hair days," those are the ones a few days past the "looking good dirty hair days."

* Mom bun (if your haircut allows). We moms can't be held back by getting wisps of hair in our faces. We have sh*t to do!

* Hair tie on the wrist. For the inevitable ponytail or mom bun. As a mom, your hair is usually in variations of ponytail or bun…unless you're just coming from the salon. Then milk that blowout for all it's worth, girl!

* Cross-body bag or backpack. For hands-free action. You need your hands freed up to catch falling cups or toddlers with your ninja skills. Plus, your kids make you carry all of their crap, so you can't be tied down.

* Sunglasses. Sunglasses are a girl's best friend. Up all night with the toddler? Don't sweat it, sunglasses got you covered. Instant Hollywood glamour!

Look, many occupations call for wearing a uniform. My mom, who worked in the restaurant business, wore bow ties, vests, and tuxedo shirts my whole childhood. When she was home with me, she only ever wore black clothes. In fact, I don't think I've ever seen my mother in anything except black and white. So as modern moms, we don't have the lock on uniforms, but we may have just perfected it.

ILLUSTRATION OF PROPERLY DEPLOYED MOM UNIFORM

☑ YOGA PANTS

☑ T-SHIRT

☑ SNEAKERS

☑ SUNGLASSES

☑ HAIR TIED BACK

☑ BACKPACK

#56. THE STUFF YOU EAT (BECAUSE I REFUSE TO USE THE WORD DIET)

Food. We need it to live, get up out of bed, and chase our rugrats. Sometimes we overindulge and then regret it. The stuff you eat is key to your overall health and well-being. It's easy to fall into the trap of finishing the last of the fries, the second half of the PB&J sandwich, or the remnants of the chicken nuggies. Of course, they are delicious; they were engineered that way! I won't lecture you on your macros or achieving ketosis and clean eating. The internet is *full* of people who will tell you to "eat this, not that!" I am here to say: find balance in the stuff you eat. If you find yourself eating the leftovers of the mac and cheese with an extra-large serving spoon over the sink three days a week, you may need to evaluate where you can make a healthier choice.

Dietary needs also change based upon your lifestyle. Pregnant? You may need an additional 300 calories per day on top of the 1800–2000 the average woman requires. Nursing? Your body may require even more. Nothing sheds pounds like starting your own dairy farm!

The extra calories that you consume while nursing should not cause weight gain as long as you're making healthy choices. As your body makes breast milk, it burns off those extra calories. If you're eating a healthy, well-balanced diet, you should gradually lose your pregnancy weight. *But* if you are chowing down on junk foods or empty calorie treats, the weight will come off more slowly or even increase. Focus on the nutrients your body needs to either make the baby or feed the baby, depending where you are.

Drink *lots* of water. Eat whole, nutritious foods. Leave the goldfish crackers for the lil ones and those diet teas for whatever BS Instagram influencer drinks them. (Damn it! I said I wasn't going to say diet, "the word that must not be named!")

Whatever your current place in the ongoing challenge that is nutrition, be kind to yourself and set achievable goals. Body positivity is more than just a trendy phrase. It's a lifestyle.

Claire Mysko, body-image expert and author of *You're Amazing! A No-Pressure Guide to Being Your Best Self*, reminds us that we need to reframe how to talk about body shaming. When your bestie down talks herself, don't jump in and reply "No way! You're amazing in that dress!" Let's be honest, we've *all* done it! We should offer a new concept, "You deserve to feel awesome in your body, and it sucks that we're taught to believe beauty and health have one look, which is total BS!" By connecting with our friends on a deeper level rather than reinforcing social norms on body types, we can commend them for being awesome people with positive, inspirational attitudes. And we can support each other in making healthy food choices.

 To learn more about healthy eating, visit:

* www.choosemyplate.gov - Choose My Plate from the USDA is full of recipes and useful facts.

#57. Activities Loosely Resembling Exercise

Motherhood itself can be a workout. That's why we wear yoga pants! Bending to pick up toys, carrying the babies (and older kids when they're tired), running to stop the toddler from jumping off the counter, and cleaning up crumbs on your hands and knees under the table are all examples of how moms move their bodies every single day. Don't ever be hard on yourself for wearing workout clothes and not going to the gym. You're *at* the gym now.

Your home (yes, with the kids inside) can be your own personal gym. You can do squats while the kids watch Paw Patrol. You can plank while they are playing Hot Wheels. You can do mountain climbers while they play LOL Dolls. Getting on the floor and getting active while they play is a great way to spend time with them (and get out of actually having to play pretend). I will say I am a much better mother in terms of mobility and energy when I am engaged actively in my own fitness. Try to get three solid days a week of exercise to clear your head and maintain your physical vigor. Your kids will appreciate a mama who can jump on the trampoline with them, and you will appreciate not getting sore every time you're asked to race to the car.

Wanna kill two birds with one stone? Find a workout partner who you enjoy spending time with. Working out with a friend promotes accountability because you don't want to let her down and you don't want to let yourself down in the process. It also helps to choose someone who won't be mad if you need to cancel at the last minute and vice versa. Life happens. Plus, it's an ear to listen when you're struggling on your journey—either in fitness or motherhood.

So put on your workout clothes (you're likely already wearing them), throw back your hair (also probably already done), grab some water and your bestie, and let's get physical!

Home Workout Routine

(No equipment needed unless you want to use a Tonka truck as a weight. Those are *heavy*!):

1.) Pretend you're a bridge so your kid can drive cars under you. (Plank for 30 seconds)

2.) Pretend you're an elevator and give your kid a ride. (Push-ups: 30 reps)

3.) Pretend you're a rocket ship and blast off. (Lunges: 10 each leg)

4.) Pretend you're sitting on a whoopie cushion. (Squats: 20 reps)

5.) Play peek-a-boo. (Sit-ups: 30 reps)

Repeat two times or until your kids start screaming for you to bring them snacks.

#58. Where U At?: Loss of Identity

Do you feel like you lost yourself in motherhood? It's a common feeling. I asked Dr. Ashurina Ream, clinical psychologist and founder of Psyched Mommy to dive into the concept of loss of identity many mothers feel. Let's take a minute to review her insights and reflect on these thoughts.

The motherhood identity crisis is real, and it may sound like:

* My body doesn't feel familiar.
* I'm just a mom.
* How can I be a mom and a partner?
* I used to have a social life.
* I don't feel connected to my friends.
* I don't do anything important.
* Once upon a time I had goals.
* Who am I?
* I used to be so driven.
* How can I balance work and home?
* My days all blend together.

An identity crisis presents a time of role confusion. Often we experience this when we undergo a period of major transition. Parenthood creates a big shift in our identity, and it happens overnight. If you're feeling disconnected from your previous self and questioning "Who am I?" I suggest exploring new or old activities of interest to you. Here are a few examples:

* Writing
* Team sports
* Yoga
* Singing

* Reading
* Poetry
* Cooking
* Crafting
* Gardening
* Blogging
* Investing
* Advocacy
* Community building

Reflection: Despite the sense of loss and changing identity, what have you found about yourself? What skills have you acquired or strengthened?

If you continue to feel like you lost yourself, don't be afraid to seek out professional help from a therapist. Remember, you're still you, and maybe now with newfound skills.

#59. Mommy Wine Culture

We've all seen the jokes. "They whine. I wine." "It's a pump and dump kinda day." "It's Wine o'clock!" You see the quippy shirts at Marshalls and the "Rosé All Day" pillows at HomeGoods. You get the picture.

At first, the mommy wine jokes were funny, and then they quickly devolved into a stale trope about modern parenting. The cultural pendulum swung hard and fast. Mommy Wine Culture is a slippery slope because you don't want to look like a square. Is that even a term anymore? Where's Urban Dictionary when I need it?!

Why does it matter?

The mommy wine jokes may seem innocent enough on the surface, but they can be insidious. Mommy Wine Culture may compound problems mamas face because it encourages us to avoid or escape reality, while encouraging a sense of helplessness. It may send a message that moms can't cope with their feelings productively. It may promote numbing uncomfortable feelings and worse, may show our children that a person needs alcohol to cope with the struggles of daily life or that the children's behavior is to blame for Mom's drinking.

Please do not think that every mom has a glass of wine after she puts the kids to bed. Please don't think it's what you "should be doing" now that you're a mom. Just like you shouldn't buy into the hype of perfect Instagram families, don't buy into the hype that everybody drinks. And get this, heavy drinking becomes an issue at some point in the lives of 71 percent of white women, 47 percent of Black women, 47 percent of Hispanic women, and 37 percent of Asian women (National Institute on Alcohol Abuse and Alcoholism). Women who abuse alcohol are at risk for basically everything and die at a rate twice as high as men who abuse alcohol. Even moderate wine drinking can be a form of self-medication. It may be used to relieve stress in the short term but doesn't promote long-term coping strategies.

There's nothing wrong with the occasional glass of wine. But if you see it's becoming an issue, it's ok to seek help. Don't take the trope to mean it's expected of you or ok for your health.

You are categorically not alone in your experience. There is no shame in speaking with a medical professional or joining a female-only Alcoholics Anonymous meeting. Your kids will thank you for being there for them.

Check out:

* Read *Bottled: A Mom's Guide to Early Recovery* by Dana Bowman
* Read *The Sober Diaries: How One Woman Stopped Drinking and Started Living* by Clare Pooley

#60. SHAME ON YOU, MOM-SHAMERS

"Did you see the way she was holding her baby?"

"She ignores her kids at the playground because she's always on her phone."

"She feeds her kids boxed macaroni and cheese!"

Mom-shaming is a frequently tossed around word. What does it mean? Let's break it down, shall we?

What?

Mom-shaming is when a person criticizes a mom (or dad) for their parenting choices because they differ from the choices that the shamer would make. These snap judgments oftentimes come from a place of complete ignorance and just plain sh*tiness.

Where?

Mom-shaming happens in real life and online. Celebrities, like Chrissy Teigen, are very often victims of mom-shaming on social media. Closer to home, it's the snide comment from the lady at the supermarket or derogatory social media comments from that mean girl from middle school. Why is she still so mean?!?

How?

Mothers are a vulnerable group because they are stressed out with a minivan full of responsibilities. Shamers pick on an unprotected group, like bullies in a schoolyard.

Why?

Shamers do it for a variety of reasons. They want to impart what they think is the best way to do something, whether it's how to educate children or canning peaches. They may genuinely want to contribute to a conversation without giving adequate thought about the feelings of the recipient. Alternatively, they want to make themselves feel better about their own life choices. Mom-shaming is often disguised as "helpful advice" albeit unsolicited or often unhelpful.

What to do about it?

Empathy. Empathy. Empathy. Have empathy for others. Do not engage in mom-shaming!

Remember mom-shaming can go both ways. When you are tempted to do it online or in real life, keep your thoughts to yourself. Keep it movin'. Keep scrolling. You never know what the other mom is going through on any given day.

That mom on the cell phone while her kids run amok? She's actually busy handling her father's funeral arrangements. That mom at the supermarket with the kids on her arm buying non-organic food that you would never buy your own kids? She just lost her job and has no access to childcare right now.

Since you don't know all sides of the story, choose to be on the side of kindness.

Also, if and when you're the recipient of mom-shaming, know that you are a good mom and do not listen to haters. Hold your head high and know this, too, shall pass.

"HERE'S SOME ADVICE" CHART

Percentage of Times Unsolicited Advice is Helpful
4.8%

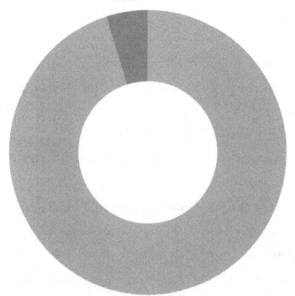

Percentage of Times Unsolicited Advice is Unhelpful
95.2%

#61. THERE'S A MOM CODE. WHY DIDN'T ANYONE TELL ME?

The mom code is a collection of unspoken rules for modern motherhood. It's often simply an understood notion with a wink and a nod; however, since this is a guidebook, I would be remiss if I didn't break it down for you.

1. *Thou shalt forgive one another's kids for being a--holes to each other and also police thine own children from displaying a--hole-ish behavior.*

2. *Thou shalt plan girls' night out (GNO) events that wrap up before 11:00 PM, late enough so the kids are probably asleep, but early enough so that you do not miss a minute of sleep.*

3. *Thou shalt not confuse a playdate with babysitting unless prior agreement is established, nor will the playdates be spread out in unequal fashion. When at all possible, bring provisions to said playdate, such as chips, cookies, or coffee. These considerations notwithstanding, drop-and-go shall be encouraged and accepted freely once the above have been previously established.*

4. *Thou shalt regularly compliment the other mom's parenting, cooking, or personal style. Kindness shall be the major currency among mothers adhering to the code.*

5. *Thou shalt be understanding of canceled playdates, GNOs, coffee meet-ups, and walks around the park. Life happens.*

6. *Thou shalt never allow for the introduction of glitter, slime, whistles, loud toys, or mud into a playdate or gift.*

7. *Thou shalt not brag endlessly about your child, for fear of shaming the other mother. If you are doing this, you are not practicing kindness.*

8. *Thou shalt be inclusive and welcome new mom friends into the mom group provided they have fulfilled most of the duties of the code ahead of time.*

9. *Thou shalt respect the mom uniform; however, working moms get a pass since they cannot reasonably change on the way from work. Other opportunities for deviating from the uniform include double dates, GNOs, school functions, and other occasions wherein elegant or semi-professional dress would otherwise be the norm.*

10. *Thou shalt refrain from gossip as much as possible. Gossips violate the mom code, plus nobody trusts a gossip.*

Follow the code and you're golden.

#62. Welcome to the Menagerie of Parenting Styles

At the end of the twentieth century, parenting labels, like Helicopter Parent, cropped up. Now into the twenty-first century, the Helicopter Parent has made way for a menagerie of parenting labels. New types crop up all time, making it difficult to keep track. Grab your binoculars and some popcorn! We're going to the zoo.

Helicopter Parent:

Child-development researchers Foster Cline and Jim Fay coined the term in 1990 for parents who "hover" and may be overly-involved in their children's lives, preventing their offspring from developing the necessary skills to make appropriate decisions and cope with hardships effectively. These parents paved the way for the more modern Lawnmower parents.

Lawnmower Parent (Also see: Bulldozer or Snowplow parent):

These parents "mow down" a clear path for their children by removing all obstacles that may challenge them. This parent not only helps their child with homework, but also makes sure it's correct before submitting it. Just like a lawnmower, this parenting style can be sharp and cut down the confidence, decision-making, and skill level of the child leading into adulthood.

One recent poll by the *New York Times* and Morning Consult found a majority of parents in the US were "robbing" their kids of adulthood. The poll, which looked at data from 1,508 young adults and 1,136 parents of children that age, found a majority of parents were still doing mundane tasks for their adult children. The poll found 76 percent of parents reminded their adult children of deadlines at school, 74 percent made appointments for them (including doctor's appointments), and 15 percent of parents texted or called their children to wake them up every morning. The poll also found 11 percent of parents called their children's place of work if there was an issue and 16 percent wrote a part of all of their children's job or internship applications. A poll of just me revealed, "Awwww, hell no!"

Lawnmower parenting can prevent young people from learning basic life skills, which may result in poor coping strategies, mental health issues, financial difficulties, relationship problems, time management, and even hygiene issues. Watch your fingers, folks! This one has a sharp side!

Tiger Parent:

This parent values academic excellence, strong work habits, and "college-bound" extracurriculars (even from a very early age) above leisure/unstructured time. These parents have high expectations for their children's accomplishments and their children's ability to rise to the occasion, giving them the skills for future success. Amy Chua, author of *Battle Hymn of the Tiger Mother*, who coined the phrase, once threatened to burn her daughter's toys when she failed to master a piano piece. This achievement-driven, obedience-based parenting style isn't for everyone, but it can be effective with the right kids.

Elephant Parent:

The converse to the Tiger parent is the soft and gentle Elephant parent who values emotional security and connection above achievement. A phrase coined by writer Priyanka Sharma-Sindhar, Elephant parents focus on nurturing and protecting their young children to foster bonding, strength, and confidence through the relationship.

Dolphin Parent:

In her book *The Dolphin Way: A Parent's Guide to Raising Healthy, Happy, and Motivated Kids—Without Turning into a Tiger*, Shimi Kang writes about Dolphin parents who seek collaboration, flexibility, and balance to gently guide children to success and happiness. This parenting style derives its name from the intelligent, playful, happy, highly social dolphin. Kang created the acronym POD as the three pillars defining the style. P for play and exploration, O for others, and D for downtime, which includes rest, exercise, and sleep. A nice balance, for sure.

Panda Parent:

The term dubbed by Esther Wojcicki, author of *How to Raise Successful People: Simple Lessons for Radical Results*, Panda parenting gives children freedom to make decisions for themselves (within reason), if that means walking to school alone or quitting the soccer team when it no longer sparks joy. Panda parents allow children to do things for themselves without getting in the way. The main purpose is to build the scaffolding so children can be free to make their own choices. Panda parenting allows children to be more independent and pick up responsibilities at a younger age, like packing a lunch bag or making their bed. Esther Wojcicki also uses an acronym TRICK: Trust, Respect, Independence, Collaboration, and Kindness.

Free-Range Parent:

Similar to Panda parenting, Free-range parenting, a term coined by Lenore Skenazy in her book *Free-Range Kids: Giving Our Children the Freedom We Had Without Going Nuts with Worry,* promotes independence and self-reliance. Whether it means playing at the playground alone or walking to school, Skenazy contends the greater risk is not allowing your children the freedom to explore independently. Often controversial, this parenting style is a throwback to the upbringing of previous generations. Their website, www.letgrow.org is pretty great, whatever your opinion on this style, and I highly recommend visiting it.

Lighthouse Parent:

Lighthouse parenting is a term coined by Dr. Kenneth Ginsburg in his book *Raising Kids to Thrive.* Parents should be lighthouses for their children, solid symbols visible from the shoreline like a beacon of light. There are two main principles of lighthouse parenting: giving unconditional love and letting children fail. More hands-on than Free-range parenting, Lighthouse parenting offers more guidance and focuses on effort and not necessarily performance.

Phew!

Whether you identify with an animal or with heavy machinery, it's ok for parents to change their parenting style over time or adopt multiple styles. As parents, we are not obligated to be one or all of them individually, culturally, or socially. Based upon our situations and even our children's temperaments, we have to remain flexible in our approaches.

Personally, I have evolved as a parent over the years from a Helicopter parent to more of an Elephant/Panda-ish (heavy on the -ish part)/Lighthouse one. Every day, I work on fostering my child's independence while tiptoeing to take a backseat on my neediness to control situations, because I know, in the long run, it's not beneficial for him. I had a tremendous amount of independence and personal responsibility as a child and looking back, I'm grateful for it. I also know my kid. If I only focused on achievements, he'd crumble under the pressure and internalize it all as failure. Your kids are individual people; try to meet them halfway and consider that these styles may not be one-size-fits-all.

#63. THE MENTAL LOAD OF MOTHERHOOD: HEAVY WEIGHS THE CROWN

Buying birthday gifts for your kid's classmate. RSVPing to said birthday party. Moving the laundry from the washer to the dryer. Remembering to buy hot sauce. Bringing oranges for the soccer game. Managing the family's calendar. Sending your in-laws an anniversary card. Finishing that work email to your client. Remembering sunscreen and your kid's swim vest. Knowing when the next doctor's appointment is scheduled. The list could fill the rest of this book... wait, gotta go, I left a pot of water boiling and need to throw some pasta in there!

Ok, I'm back! The mental load of motherhood is all-encompassing. It's all the stuff. If we aren't the ones remembering it, it often doesn't get done. Meaning, it never gets done.

Did you ever notice this phenomenon? Moms are always the last ones in the car because they are running around the house grabbing all of the things that no one else thinks to grab. And if they forget something like towels, *one* time, that's when everybody remembers it!

Motherhood is packing up all of your family's stuff for the beach and forgetting your own bathing suit. Been there, done that!

As mothers, we are the center with the spokes sprouting out from us on the wheel of life. We are the ones holding everything together and making everything flow smoothly (as smoothly as real life can flow). But, we wear out after a while. Being the wheel and keeping it in motion is exhausting!

If the mental load is becoming too heavy for you to bear, here are some suggestions for unloading it:

* Ask for help, even when it's hard. At first, it may seem easier to do things yourself. But over time, the weight can become unbearable for one person. This is when you have to ask your partner, a friend, another family member, or your children for assistance. It's likely your partner wants to help and doesn't know how. Show them. Tell them. Walk them through it.

* Instead of asking your partner to do certain chores, which frames you more as a household manager and your partner an underling, ask your partner to take on certain responsibilities. "Can you be in charge of buying gifts for the birthday parties?" "Can you put a reminder on your calendar to keep an eye on that every Tuesday?"

* Help your partner open their eyes as to what needs to be done. Like the rogue Cheerio on the floor or the laundry needing to be carried upstairs, sometimes all you have to do is point it out. With deliberate practice, this behavior will hopefully spread to other areas in your life, such as making doctor's appointments, attending school events, or buying their parents an anniversary card.

* Get the children to participate too. Periodt.

You're a mom who can do it all, but you don't have to do it all, all the time.

THE MENTAL LOAD OF MOTHERHOOD

*Word cloud taken from writings of @modernmomprobs comments

#64. THE BALANCING ACT OF MOTHERHOOD

We've made it this far in this guide for you to know that moms are pulled in one trillion different directions, between work calls, doctor's appointments, homework, snacks, snacks, and snacks.

People often ask, "How do I balance my work, family, and play?"

Pay close attention. Are you ready? Here is the secret to finding perfect balance in your life:

1.) FORGET THAT SH*T!
2.) LET THAT SH*T GO!
3.) DISREGARD THAT SH*T!
4.) ABANDON THAT THOUGHT!
5.) IT DOESN'T ACTUALLY EXIST OR NEED TO!

First, you have to let go of the notion of complete and perfect balance. It doesn't exist; it will never exist. Important: it doesn't need to exist. Balance is a tricky and loaded term because it implies equal attention to multiple things. That's a set-up. Miss one basketball game because work went long? You're out of balance. Miss a day of work because the kids got the flu? Out of balance again.

To simplify your life, you must let certain things go, like the notion of doing it all—and effortlessly. You must focus on *effectiveness* over balance. Am I an effective boss/employee at work? Am I an effective mother at home? Am I effective at taking good care of myself? Keep these things separate and don't think they need to balance out one another. They won't. Letting certain things go may look like not cooking every meal from scratch or asking your significant other (or kids!) for help with the housework. You have to decide what effectiveness looks like to you, not whether it looks like balance.

Choose what you feel comfortable with in terms of what you want to prioritize. Don't care if your closets are a little messy as long as the rest of your home is tidy? Cool. Feel anxious when your closets are teeming with stuff? That's cool, too. Focus on what you deem important. While you're at it, focus on the positive and evaluate what you feel is an accomplishment. Did you absolutely rock a client presentation? That's because you're a rock star! Did you get chosen to be class mom? Good for you, too! Revel in the things you kick ass at!

Lastly: *Stop. The. Comparisons.* Don't compare yourself to Jessica down the street who bakes homemade organic blueberry muffins each week or Sarah who creates hair bows and works full-time and has five kids. Good for them. Ask them for tips. But don't compare yourself to them.

We can't give everything to everybody all of the time. Not only does it set you up for failure to think you have to, it's simply impossible. It's the expectations bully creeping up on you again. Find peace in knowing that you are crushing it on many fronts and are flexible enough to pivot when your attention is needed elsewhere.

So I say, let's shut down the lie we tell ourselves: that balance is the goal and is natural and is the only way you can "have it all." You know what you can have all of? You can have all the confidence that you don't need to juggle a certain amount of balls in the air to be "balanced." Let's turn this topsy-turvy and just be effective. In modern motherhood that means simply giving it your best and showing up emotionally, mentally, and physically for your kids, when you can. Have the confidence to let sh*t go when you can't. Now this seems like a good time to transition our convo to mom guilt.

#65. MOM GUILT CAN SHOVE IT

Am I doing enough?
Am I on my phone for work too often?
Are they getting too much screen time?
Too much junk food?
Not enough music lessons?

Am I spending enough time with my partner?

Is my anxiety affecting our relationship?

Everyone else seems to have their sh*t together but me. What's wrong with me?

First of all, there's nothing wrong with you if your head swims with these questions.

We all face mom guilt to one degree or another. How could we not!? We're bombarded with message upon message, forcing us to pick sides in the parenting battle and hoping that path is the "right" one. The shiny, curated images we see online reinforce our guilt because our lives don't reflect these images (I can hardly get my kid to wear pants, let alone matching outfits with my husband and me on a holiday). Mom guilt manifests when our expectations do not match our reality (expectations, there they are again). It also plays into the concept of parenting as a sport. We think a "good mom" does all the right things, is always present, and always has a huge smile on her face. I call BS!

Mom guilt is like an internal bully coming to beat you up at the playground. When it starts creeping up in the silence of your mind, tell it to go kick rocks. Send it crying home to its mama. You have no time for a clouded mind space. Life's hard enough.

I'm throwing down the gauntlet. I challenge you to change your perspective and throw away your guilt. The world has been altered since the quarantine. Parts of our modern mom culture are gone. And that's cool with me. Maybe it's better than cool; maybe it helps us gain a truer perspective. Although the quarantine felt like an eternity, it was only a blip in the scheme of your lifetime. Now's the time to simplify your life going forward. It's ok to simply "just be." If there's a lesson in there, it's "*you* are enough, Mama." Let go of the expectations you had for yourself, what you thought your kids' childhood would be like. Keeping your family happy, healthy, and safe are your top priorities—the matching outfits can wait.

When times get tough just remember, *grit over guilt.*

Quiz:

Question: Which of the following is not a sport?

A.) Soccer   B.) Baseball   C.) Curling   D.) Parenting

Answer: Duh, parenting! Though curling is close to not being a sport.

#66. I'm Tired AF: A Love Letter to Coffee

My Love,

Coffee, sweet nectar of the gods. I have no problem with you, baby. My only problem is that I can't get enough of you. I dream of you touching my lips even before I fall asleep at night. But I know I need to resist. When I muster the energy to get out of bed, I crawl into your open arms. You make me tremble with anticipation and caffeination.

Why do the corporate fat cats charge so much to keep me away from you? Is it our destiny? No, fate brings us together again and again, every morning for the rest of our lives. Thank you, you delicious, perfectly roasted, caffeinated lover.

Yours truly,
A Modern Mom

#67. Rage Cleaning Those Feelings Away

Sick of everyone's stuff everywhere? Those tiny little plastic high heels and smelly erasers all over the floor? Grab a rag, some spray, and go rage clean the living room. Oh, you don't know what rage cleaning is?

Lucky you. Let me fill you in. Rage cleaning is when you go around your house passive aggressively cleaning and stomping your feet, like the Tasmanian Devil on her period.

Rage cleaning can be triggered by a host of things: stepping on a sharp pointy toy, the constant state of messiness around you, someone making a mess after you just cleaned, feeling unappreciated, or my all-time favorite, cleaning up before company arrives with little warning.

To combat the "rage cleanies":

1. Take a deep breath in. Slowly breathe out through your nose.
2. Know that a mess does not mean you are failing.
3. Try to identify why a mess triggers you. Is it that it prevents you from thinking clearly? Is it because no one is assisting you in these duties?
4. Communicate with your family members about their responsibilities in maintaining the household. They may even…help?!?!
5. Set realistic expectations for yourself. You are only one person.
6. Set a timer on your phone for your rage cleaning. Let's say ten minutes and reevaluate after that.
7. When you're expecting company, feel free to tidy up. But more importantly, be kind to yourself because they aren't looking at your baseboards anyway. Hide all the other crap in the closet and deal with it later.

How many calories does rage cleaning burn? Not sure, but it always seems like a helluva lot.

Sometimes you need just one friend who says, "I get it. If there is anyone in the world who understands, it's me. Trust me, I get it."

Chapter 6
FRIEND PROBS

*M*oms need mom friends. They may even be more important than coffee. Maybe. This chapter is meant to help you understand friendships a bit better and help you navigate the process of finding friends. Moms need playdates, too!

#68. MAKING MOM FRIENDS (IS VITAL AND YOU SHOULD LOOK INTO IT)

When my son was first born, I had no friends with children yet. We felt like the first ones to enter this brave new world of parenting. Many moms met people for walks in the park. But my son was born at the end of November in New York City, so no one was flocking to the park for a leisurely stroll. There was no natural way to meet anybody. It was a very lonely time for me. Each day was like a count-down until my husband came home from work, so I could speak with another adult in complete sentences or listen to his stories about the outside world. Thank goodness for Netflix. *Downton Abbey* was my only friend.

Once my son started daycare, I met the other moms of his "class-mates." (I use quotation marks because it's hilarious to think of tiny, drooling infants being in a classroom setting.) Finally, I started meeting moms like me, who felt like me, and experienced motherhood like me. It was so refreshing to have friends again. I would live for the brief moments of picking up my son and seeing that one mom I really clicked with. I thought: Maybe if I run into her often enough, we can exchange numbers and we'll be *best friends forever*.

A natural extrovert and only child, I've never had an issue making new friends; however, with the addition of this new little person I created and loss of myself in my new role, this normally easy task was filled with self-doubt and reluctance. Long story short, we exchanged digits and began doing playdates at each other's homes, for which I'm eternally grateful.

My advice for making new mom friends is take a deep breath, step outside of your comfort zone, and ask that mom to hang out. You'll be so glad you did. You can meet up at the park for a picnic blanket playdate or stroll around the block together. Check out local "Mommy and Me" groups for some baby "enrichment." Keep an eye out for the mom who gets annoyed at her baby's singing performance or the mom who is trying to one-up everyone's scarf catching abilities during sing-along time.

Making mom friends with school-aged children is often easier because children meet in class or on sports teams and begin to form their own friendships. Having older children affords you the opportunity to have longer conversations with moms at pickup or during playdates. Another unintended benefit: hanging on the playground lets you observe how the kids act when playing. If their kid is sh*tty to yours even though the mom is cool, it may not be a lasting relationship. You have to gauge how much you want to invest in that relationship. Making mom friends is similar to dating except there are more interested parties involved—your kids and her kids.

Once you find the friend who clicks with you, hold on to her—not in a smothering way, more like a "let's be honest and talk about real sh*t" way. One last thing, express your gratitude to your friends. It sounds cheesy but sometimes hearing how much your friendship is valued is just the thing you need.

Wanna be friends? Check 'em out:

* Peanut app: Peanut is a social networking app to meet like-minded women.
* Local Facebook moms groups

Quiz: Is this a...friend?

So you have absorbed lots of information about mom code, mom uniforms, and some of the tropes surrounding motherhood. There's a gal in your life, you consider her a friend, but is she really a mom friend? Take the quiz below to find out.

Directions: For each question, a point value will be designated based on an aspect of friendship. Add all the points and use the scoring rubric to determine what manner of friend you are dealing with. Each "No" answer gets zero points.

1. *Would you be friends with this person if neither of you had kids? Five points*

2. *Do you have a "kid connection," such as the same classroom, activities, interests, age? Two points*

3. *Do you share similar parenting styles/views/values regarding safety, supervision, fun, and scheduling? Two points*

4. *Do your kids actually get along? Three points*
5. *Do your partners get along? One point*
6. *Is there physical proximity? Same town/neighborhood gets two points. Add a point if walkable. Same state or drives within an hour get only one point.*
7. *Do you trust one another for pickup and/or drop-off as needed? One point*
8. *Does one mom consistently have something the other has forgotten (e.g., a snack, water, tissues, band-aids) when at the playground? One point*
9. *Is there a general understanding and acceptance of messes, destruction of property, and bad behavior that would otherwise not end the friendship? One point*
10. *Are you both kind, complementary, and respectful of each other's families and personal struggles? One point*

0–5 points: Not a friend. This is at best, an acquaintance.

6–10 points: A Convenient Cathy. Your kids play the same sport in the same town, and there was that one time you gave her kid some goldfish to prevent a meltdown, but you two are just sorta kinda friends. You can be cordial, but this isn't going anywhere. She didn't even get any of the movie references you used.

11–15 points: A bud. You definitely click. And it was so cool that your kids have been reading buddies all year. But did you notice how she said nothing when her little one keyed your car? It's cool, though. She's great to be around.

16+ points: A soulmate. Sure, your husbands really have nothing in common, but this is a ride-or-die mama, a real keeper.

#69. DADS NEED FRIENDS, TOO

I have a husband. He's a nice guy, but he's a natural introvert. Happier alone. Not quick to warm up. Smart, pensive. He's social, but he's definitely the quiet one in the relationship. Dads/men are a funny bunch. Do they like people? Do they talk to one another? Should you introduce them to one another? Do they even want to know each other? It's a question moms often ask themselves at the pickup line.

If your husband (or boyfriend) is an extrovert, this is easy. He'll meet other dads and moms and take care of himself at PTO events, the playground, back to school night. But depending on which book you read, 25 to 50 percent of men are introverts, or have signs of introversion in settings where they do not feel a level of control, so what do you do with these guys? They need friends, too, they just won't admit it.

I try to introduce my husband to everybody I know at school— mom friends, "cool dads," husbands of mom friends. He's reluctant, but he has definitely become a lot more comfortable around all the other moms. And the kids love him! The unicorn introduction is when your husband gets along with a bestie's husband. I've had this work out once or twice, but it's great for both hubbies, and my friend and I get to chuckle at how cute we think the guys are together. *Bromance!* They can go on man-dates and borrow power washers and whatnot. But it's not easy to make these curmudgeony creatures get together. Just give it your best shot and know that they actually do want to make new friends, and we have to help them out.

How to Make Dad Friends (for dads):

1.) Approach fellow father/potential friend.

2.) Make the corners of your mouth go up. This is called a smile.

3.) Say "Hello, I am XYZ, YZX's husband (or So-and-so's Dad). How are you? Looks like rain, huh? The grass could use a good soaking."

4.) Discuss outdoor grills, batting averages, fresh sneakers, getting a deal at the car dealership, and the latest thermostat technology.

5.) Be glad you made a new friend.

#70. Girls' Night Out: I Did Not Know Susan Could Drink Like That

Girl's Night Out (GNO) is like chicken soup for the soul. It can get steamy, a little salty, and fills you up. After it, you feel warm and fuzzy inside; well, that could be from the margaritas. When you first have a baby, you may feel it's unfathomable to leave the baby home and go out. I did. After some time passed, I realized how much I missed the connection with other adults.

We are people, after all. We have friends. We need connections and bottomless breadsticks. So what are we waiting for? Somebody else to plan it?

GNO is the ultimate mommy playdate minus the interrupted conversations or unrelenting snack requests (unless those requests are coming from your girlfriend for more supreme nachos). We can focus on our friends, look them in the eye, and genuinely listen. People call one another by their given names and not just "Moooom."

GNO rejuvenates moms. It's our sustenance. It keeps us going. GNO makes us feel special because we shower, shave (gasp!), dress up, wear makeup, use a different purse other than the diaper bag or general carryall tote. As moms, we share battle stories, secrets, hacks, kids going through the same things, struggles with food or husbands. We share common ground. GNO is a celebration of sisterhood, even if it's only a Zoom happy hour these days.

So I say, plan that GNO now. You need it!

Recipe for the Perfect GNO:

2½ cups of laughter

¼ cup of secrets

1 cup of honesty

1½ cup of "in the trenches" stories

3 tablespoons of uninterrupted, meaningful conversations

1 lb. of greasy, fried appetizers

16 fl. oz. of yummy cocktails

A sprinkle of makeup and perfume

A dash of dancing

A pinch of a purse that's not a diaper bag

Simmer for three hours (don't overcook because you still have to wake up with the kids in the morning)

#71. THE GROUP CHAT: A CAST OF CHARACTERS

Once you solidify your group of mom friends, the next step is forming the group chat, a sacred place for plan-making and kid-bitching. Your group chat is likely filled with contacts that look like this:

AmyMax'sMom

MaryRichardsMom

NiceMomfromthepark

Neighborwiththebrowndog

Kelly

Each of the following moms are going to comprise your group chat at one point or another:

1.) The Ghoster

Also known as the Lurker. This person is over it. She's had enough of the constant banter and notifications. She doesn't particularly care what is going on, but won't leave the chat either, because she needs some of the info in the chat. She may pop in every six months or so and have a million messages to catch up on.

2). The Rapid Firer

This person is always excited about something—good or bad. She passionately texts in four-message bursts. Maybe she's a bit overexcited? Maybe she can't be bothered consolidating her thoughts into one text? Either way, get ready to hear those pings. You may want to silence your phone when she really gets going.

3.) The Novelist

This person is the opposite of the Rapid Firer. Her lengthy prose may meander, often leading you to forget this is a group chat not a book club. She has a lot to say and is going to take the time to craft her thoughts accordingly.

4.) THE ALL CAPS TYPER

OMG! THAT'S SO EXCITING AHHHH!!! She is the one who only ever speaks in caps. You can always count on her for a SUPER BIG REACTION.

5.) The Organizer

She's the planner—the one trying to organize the play dates, the PTO events, and the ladies' game night. Without her, your group of mom friends may never get together. She's a keeper.

6.) The GIF Queen

This mom always drops in at the perfect time with the perfect GIF. Whenever no one knows how to respond or what to say, this queen will come and save the day by sending a GIF to add some comedy to an awkward conversation. After all, a picture is worth a thousand words.

7.) The Emoji Dropper

This person is the group's "yes-woman." She usually just sends confirmation texts or emojis to the group that don't add anything to the conversation except for another notification. But at least you know from the well-placed thumbs up that she will be attending soccer practice tonight.

Now that you know the different types, you can plan your phone notification options accordingly.

#72. Types of Mom Friends You Have Right Now

I've said it once, and it's worth repeating. Mom friends are crucial! They listen to us when we replay our fictitious life scenarios, normally reserved for the inanimate objects in our shower. Once you find your circle of friends, see if you can identify the types of mom friends. Bear in mind, you can be one or more of these archetypes at a time and grow into or out of some of these roles as well. Just have fun with it!

The Well-Informed Mom: She has her opinions about all kinds of things—nutrition, medical care, and education. She's well-read and ready to defend her views. With her level of research, her opinions are usually, well, correct. She knows what the Board of Education is planning and what the town is doing about EVERYTHING. She knows all of the local events.

Why this mom friend is important: She's passionate about her beliefs and is really knowledgeable. She may come off as opinionated and a know-it-all, but she means well. A real keeper!

The Type-A Mom: You know the type. Intensity in ten cities. This mom is a planner. She is the master of spreadsheets, calendars, and reminders. She's always on time (even with her kids). Her kids go to bed on time every night (yes, this can happen). She's busy, super-involved, and on top of it all. Count on this mom when you have zero clue when the next PTO meeting is supposed to happen.

Why this mom friend is important: This mom has work/life effectiveness down because it's written in her calendar that way. Hanging around with her means you will always be on time when you arrive somewhere together, and you will always know what's going on (and when it's happening). Let her organization rub off on you a bit so you don't show up an hour late for the spring recital (again).

The Type-B Mom: This mama is the contrast to Type-A Mom. She won't remember sh*t. No clue about dates, doesn't write anything down, and may or may not clean up before (or after) a playdate. She's suuuuuuper chill. When she says she'll meet you for coffee at 12:00 PM, she means more like 12:25 PM because she couldn't get her life together that morning. She's most likely to call her kids "little a--holes" but also is a ton of fun.

Why this mom friend is important: She is always up for having you over at her house regardless of the state of it. She's just trying to make it through the day and wants a break. She's a great listener, great to be around, and a perfect reminder that you can have happy kids without perfection.

The Out-of-the-Loop Mom: This mom doesn't know the kids in the class or teachers that her own kids don't have. She may not be up on the mom uniform, and she usually doesn't know when school events are going to happen. She may be full of guilt over all of this stuff because it's not that she doesn't care, it's just that she has some circumstances that make it challenging.

Why this mom friend is important: She is looking to you for guidance and friendship. She desperately wants to be in the loop and may have other obligations that prevent her from doing so. Be nice to her, support her, and let her know that you know she's a great mom and you have her back.

The Crafty Mom: Not only does this mom have a Pinterest board, but she actually does the stuff on the board and posts her own pins. Beautiful birthday party decor? Done. Different door wreaths for every holiday? Uh-huh. Homemade wooden signs for her dining room? Yep. Chalkboard signs for the first day of school? Check. Has a Cricut for making custom birthday shirts every year? Bingo. This mom is unapologetically crafty, artsy, creative, however you want to say it (and I wish some rubbed off on me).

Why this mom friend is important: She's ultra-creative. She's the mom you can look to for the best Halloween costumes because she's teeming with ideas. Your kid wants to be a mailbox for Halloween? She's your girl. Just realize, she is not doing this to one-up any other parent. She's just doing what makes her happy and to make special memories for her children. Don't compare yourself to her. Maybe she can help you out and make that mailbox costume for your kid (because you should probably not attempt).

The Mentor Mom: This mama has seen it all. She may be juggling at least three or more children in different grades, different schools, and different extracurricular activities. She may even have older kids and a baby at the same time. She knows which teachers are the "best" ones to get each year. She loves to impart her wisdom to the new moms.

Why this mom friend is important: She's like having an older sister who can offer sound advice. Since her experience covers a lot of ground, she can provide several different perspectives. Information is her currency.

The Ride-or-Die Mom: This friend is your to-go. The one you can count on. You can always trust her to be down for adventures. She's up for anything you throw at her. Want to toss the kid in the car and drive to the zoo on short notice? Let's go. Does she buy a six-foot beach ball for her backyard kiddie pool and pick up your kids for an epic playdate? Yep. She is fun and trustworthy. She's most likely to be the school emergency contact for your children. You and your kid are having a rough day? She has the right words and zero judgment.

Why this mom friend is important: This mama is trustworthy through and through—as a pal and a confidant (Golden Girls reference fully intended). You can trust her with your secrets and even your children's lives. This mom is a treasure.

The Modern Mom: This mom is a healthy combination of some or all of the above. She's authentic, she's down to earth, and she knows she's not perfect (nor are her children). She knows parenting is a crapshoot every day. This mom is sympathetic, kind, fun, inclusive, and enjoys laughing.

Why this mom friend is important: The modern mom is all of us, and we are important.

PROGRESSION OF
Date Night

- Over the 1st drink, you discuss the kids

- Over the 2nd drink, you discuss the house

- Over the 3rd drink, you start to loosen up

- Over the 4th drink, you discuss moving to

Hawaii to sell shave ice by the side of the road

Chapter 1
RELATIONSHIP PROBS

*M*arriage while Parenting: Proceed with Caution. This chapter lays out the nuances of relationships, the importance of working together, and the different types of modern families all facing different kinds of problems.

#73. Syncing Those Parenting Styles to Advance World Peace

So you and your partner have adopted, fostered, or created a human life and made it through both the "keep mushy baby alive" and "keep running crazy person alive" phases. Now let's say you have kids between ages two and thirty-two. You want to know the odds that the two of you agree on every parenting topic coming your way? Pretty, pretty, pretty low.

In fact, you may be lucky if you see eye-to-eye on half of all the parenting decisions you will make. Earlier in the book we took a little tour of the various parenting styles, but now you have to sync it up. Have to. As in, you must. This doesn't mean you won't play good cop, bad cop from time to time. You will. But if you want to survive as a couple, you have to consider the strain child-raising will have on you and how much conflict small disagreements can cause.

Nearly every study of the reasons for divorce has pinned the main drivers as including some combination of constant conflict, infidelity, incompatibility, drinking or drug use, and/or growing apart. I can't help you if your partner is unfaithful or if they have a substance problem. But let me tell you, if you want to avoid the other problems like constant conflict, feelings of incompatibility, or a feeling of growing apart, you should sit down and deliberately discuss how you will present a unified front to your kid(s). We do it all the time, and it saves us any relationship contact we might otherwise have.

Think about scenarios that have happened in your family already. Think about things that have not yet happened. And decide what works for your family. It's better to hash it out and come to an agreement than learn through very heavy conflict that you truly aren't on the same page when it comes to the amount of screen time you think is allowable. Deliberately staying out ahead of such issues and being constructive with each other is tremendously helpful. If I slip on something, like making sure our son works on his handwriting before he can play Pokémon Go, my husband can call me on it, and vice versa. It doesn't lead to a fight because we are a team and need to be accountable to one another so our family thrives.

So, seek alignment as a couple. You'll send more consistent messages to the kiddos, and you will have one less thing to fight about. That's a win in my book.

Parenting issues to talk about and agree upon (to make your life easier):
* Bedtime
* Screen time (TV, video games)
* Mealtime
* Manners
* Grades
* Punishment
* Explicit language
* Extracurricular activities
* Chores
* Mental health and developmental issues

#74. DATE NIGHT: THE LIFE'S BLOOD OF KEEPING IT TOGETHER

Ok, you finally did it. You called Mom or got a babysitter and it's time for date night. You have a lot of choices, so choose wisely. This list could literally be hundreds of activities long, but there are word limits and you're busy! I tried to keep it as budget conscious as possible because these kids are costing you enough moolah already.

1. Take a hike: Get on those hiking boots and pack a lunch. Also bring some bug repellent and remind yourself of what poison ivy looks like.

2. Sit in your car and eat some tacos: Workouts are nice, but chicken burritos are also nice. Not your idea of a hot date? Fine, but don't be all judgy about it!

3. Stay at home and make some popcorn for a movie night: Netflix and chill has now become very cliché, but really isn't that all you want sometimes?

4. Fix yourself a drink and look at the stars: Get outside, get buzzed, and enjoy the wonders and immensity of space.

5. Take a nice long drive: Pick a scenic route or at the very least an easy drive with not a lot of stop and go. Crank the music. Destination is optional.

6. Do something new: Sounds vague, but I guarantee there are things you haven't tried or places you have never been together. When's the last time you played mini golf as a couple? An escape room? Axe throwing? Maybe you'll find your new hobby or passion together.

7. Go to dinner but do that thing where you sit on the same side of the booth: You know what I'm talking about. Already do that? Welp, time to sit across from one another.

8. Learn something new: Cooking classes are awesome. You should try one.

9. Work out: Feeling healthy? Pick an activity that you can properly do together without your husband gloating that he can dunk a basketball and you cannot.

10. Have an at-home adventure: Give your kid the iPad, sneak into the bathroom, lock the door, and have sex. See you next chapter….

#75. Keepin' It Spicy (Intimacy)

The average married couple has sex approximately *I don't care* number of times a week. The right amount and type of intimacy is something only you and your partner can define. I am, by no means, an expert in this arena, but I present to you the bottom line, single-word solution to any intimacy challenges my husband and I have ever had: communication! You have to talk about intimacy at this point in your life. It's just not going to happen spontaneously like it once did. Sorry.

You aren't kids anymore. Your hormones are much more settled. You're tired from work and from having kids hanging all over you all day. Even if you want to go, there's homework to do and snacks to fetch. But you have to keep your intimacy alive to maintain connection as a couple.

If that sounds like work, it kind of is. I'm sorry to dispel any illusions you may be holding onto regarding the amorous realities of marriage. But I promise you, scheduling in some private couple time won't make it any less exciting. Hold hands more often, talk about your needs, and just block out all the other distractions to focus on one another for a change. You made some beautiful kids; you both deserve to be treated nicely.

Secret Code to Intimacy Game

Use the letters on the left to decode letters on the right.

___ __ __ __ __ __ __ __ __ __ __ __ __ __ __ __ __ __

J K F G 4 F 9 E 7   G L Q Q C 5 J   1 E 4

__ __ __ __ __ __ __ __ __

7 F   8 1 M 5   J 5 O

1=A	6=F	B=K	G=P	L=U
2=B	7=G	C=L	H=Q	M=V
3=C	8=H	D=M	I=R	N=W
4=D	9=I	E=N	J=S	O=X
5=E	A=J	F=O	K=T	P=Y
				Q=Z

ANSWER: STOP DOING PUZZLES AND GO HAVE SEX.

#76. BUILDING A HOUSE WITH NO CLOSETS: PARENTING AN LGBTQ+ KID

I have talked a lot about expectations throughout this book. But, most of the expectations we have as parents are for the things our kids can *do*. That's a lot of pressure, but we've all experienced it, so sometimes it's like, "suck it up." I get it.

Now imagine the pressure you'd feel about not living up to your parents' expectations not for what you can do, but for *who you are*. Seems like an impossibly crushing experience, doesn't it?

So just as you need to lower your expectations that Junior isn't going to be a superstar quarterback in the NFL, you should also change your expectations for their gender and sexual preferences. I'm serious. Do it now.

It's a silly thing to even think about though, isn't it? You want your son/daughter to grow up and have sex a certain way? It's their business. They wouldn't weigh in on your sex life as adults.

Why does this matter? Raising an LGBTQ+ kid is the same as any typical kid, right? Well, yes and no. Unless you have been willfully ignorant, you will have seen the stories of young kids (alarmingly young) who have turned to drugs or alcohol or committed suicide because they (and/or their families) could not come to accept their sexuality. Your parenting process and messaging will affect how accepted your child feels.

Make your house one driven by acceptance, and signal to your children, with every opportunity you get, that you will love them *no matter who they are*. Signal to them that they can tell you what's going on in their mind or in their hearts…no matter what. We want them to worry about cleaning their frickin' rooms and not worry about whether they will be disowned because of their emerging sexual preference.

The Trevor Project (www.thetrevorproject.org) is a great resource for parents. It's a "national organization providing crisis intervention and suicide prevention services to lesbian, gay, bisexual, transgender, queer & questioning LGBTQ+ young people under twenty-five."

Some data to be aware of (directly from their site), lest you wonder why you need to get your sh*t together on this topic right now:

*   Suicide is the second leading cause of death among young people ages ten to twenty-four.
*   LGB youth who come from highly rejecting families are 8.4 times as likely to have attempted suicide as LGB peers who reported no or low levels of family rejection.
*   LGB youth seriously contemplate suicide at three times the rate of heterosexual youth.
*   LGB youth are almost five times as likely to have attempted suicide compared to heterosexual youth.
*   Of all the suicide attempts made by youth, LGB youth suicide attempts were almost five times as likely to require medical treatment than those of heterosexual youth.
*   Suicide attempts by LGB youth and questioning youth are four to six times more likely to result in injury, poisoning, or overdose that requires treatment from a doctor or nurse, compared to their straight peers.
*   In a national study, 40 percent of transgender adults reported having made a suicide attempt. Ninety-two percent of these individuals reported having attempted suicide before the age of twenty-five.

* Each episode of LGBT victimization, such as physical or verbal harassment or abuse, increases the likelihood of self-harming behavior by 2.5 times on average.

Make the conscious effort to create a home of love and acceptance because in the end, that is what family is all about.

To learn more, check out:
* www.glaad.org - GLAAD leads the conversation for LGBTQ+ acceptance. It offers valuable resources for parents and youth.
* www.pflag.org - PFLAG connects LGBTQ+ families for peer support and education.

#77. OZZIE AND HARRIET DON'T LIVE HERE ANYMORE: THE NON-TRADITIONAL PARENTAL UNIT

Howdy there, my lesbian mom friend! How are you doing, my non-binary Zaza who chose to conceive via IVF without a partner? Heya, cis-hetero mom with a cis-hetero husband at home! What's shakin? I want you all to know I see you—and, uh, you got a Cheerio in your hair, so, uh, let me get that for you.

This is a quick reminder that moms come in all shapes, sizes, and types, and we're united in our common goal of raising good kids who will thrive in the modern world.

Parental units have *changed*, and the improved visibility of diverse family constructs in the media and our neighborhoods means the non-Ozzie and Harriets are seeing better integration into most communities. But, I fully acknowledge most of this book's readership will be from a more traditional hetero family type, so I can't emphasize enough that allyship is key. And the time is now.

So what can you do as a straight mom?

* Explain to your kids that love looks like you and daddy, but it also looks like So-and-so's two mommies as well. Families are about love. Period.

* If your kids are a bit more, ahem, advanced, explain to them that there is more than one way to become a parent. That stork gets around whether you have a mommy and daddy or not.

* Correct grandma (or your straight friend) if she shakes her head and comments, "That's going to be hard for those kids" or, "That's not right." Simply say, "No clear differences have been observed between household types and child outcomes." Or, "We're raising our kids to be accepting of all people, especially since we know that as long as kids are loved, they turn out fine." Alternatively, "Go crawl back under your rock" works wonders.

* Do not perpetuate stereotypes and certainly don't portray these families as "other" to your kids.

* If a kid doesn't have a mom and a dad and you don't know what to call the parents, ask them! It's ok, and far better than assuming "mom" is even the preferred title. Ok, maybe it feels a bit awkward for you, so wait it out a few play dates if that's better. But it's always a great way to start a conversation by saying, "I am so happy we're all friends now, and I value our friendship so I want to get this right. What are your preferred parenting titles and pronouns?" I once asked this, and the other mom was tearful because she just appreciated that I cared.

* Respect the stress that these parenting units may be under. They don't have it easy because heteronormativity is especially intense in parenting circles, and they are left on the outs in many ways. Do your part to end that.

* Invite these moms into your circle! Be an ally by actually being a friend.

There's nuance here, but being kind is not rocket science! And hey, if you won't be kind, they are gonna walk around with that Cheerio in their hair all day.

What are you waiting for?

A 2014 paper from the American Sociological Association found that in ten years of research on the subject and over forty published studies there was a clear consensus that children raised by same-sex couples fared as well as children raised by opposite-sex couples. This included academics, development, mental health, and substance abuse. The authors noted that differences in child well-being were largely due to socioeconomic circumstances and family stability.

STILL PARENTS

#78. DIVORCE HAPPENS: HOW TO RISE UP

Hey, sometimes things just don't work out. It's ok. There's one hundred million reasons why some marriages don't work. The important thing isn't why but how. How are you going to move on to bigger and better things? How are you going to put the past behind you to focus on your children, your career, and yourself?

I asked my friend Michelle Dempsey-Multack for advice about how. Michelle is a co-parent, writer, coach devoted to supporting women after divorce, and "Moms Moving On" podcast host. Because she is my go-to for all things single mamas, she provided her Top Ten Tips for Divorced and Single Mamas.

1. Pick your battles

   You now have to parent from a distance with someone who you couldn't work out a marriage with, so there will most definitely be battles. Fight the ones that mean the most to you and your child's well-being, and let the rest go.

2. Know your worth

   Just because this marriage did not work out, does not mean you are any less worthy of receiving love. Your worth is not determined by the things in your life that didn't work out, but how you move past these obstacles sure does define your strength. And strong is very, very sexy.

3. Find your people

   You may have a million friends who adore you, but if they haven't been through a divorce or raised a child on their own, chances are, they don't understand you. Your perspective is different now. Your experiences will not be the same as that of a married person. Just one friend who has "been there" is enough. Find that person, and never let her go.

4. Speaking of perspective…

    If yours is more "why me?" than "what now?", it's time for a major perspective shift. Divorce and single motherhood is hard enough as it is without the added pressure of feeling sorry for yourself. Think with your "what now?" mindset and remember how powerful this will be for your children to witness!

5. Strong mamas, strong children

    Divorce doesn't ruin children—but our behavior after the divorce can. If you're constantly upset, stressed, or tense, your children will feel it. If you're openly angry at their father, this will undoubtedly come back to bite you in the ass. Be the person you want your child to be, even if it means crying into a pillow once they're asleep.

6. Don't be afraid to ask for help

    In the way of therapy, in the way of a babysitter giving you a few hours to yourself so you can breathe, in the way of asking your best friend's husband over to help you move heavy furniture or fix a leaky faucet. Don't be afraid to ask for help.

7. Take your self-care seriously

    I don't mean manicures and fancy spa visits. I mean, know you when you need a time-out, and give it to yourself. Know that a quick walk around your neighborhood to clear your head can sometimes feel medicinal. Know that you need to take care of yourself in order to get through life as a single or divorced mama.

8. Co-parent with a child-centered approach

   If you're co-parenting with your ex, make life easier and follow a child-centered approach to decision-making. The only question you should consider when going head-to-head with your ex is, "Is this in the best interest of my child?"

9. Have your ex's best interests at heart, too

   No, seriously. If your ex is still in the picture and is involved with your child(ren), make him or her an ally. You don't have to be in love and married to get along. Let your children see how adults overcome their differences by getting along, spending time together in small increments at a child's baseball game or birthday party, and making the waters friendlier so your children never have to be scared of the next shark attack.

10. Find the good in every day

    Maybe you didn't want your divorce. Maybe you didn't want to parent on your own. But you're here now, so you may as well make the most of it. Find something good in every day—even on the hardest of days. Write it down, reread it when you're sad, and pretty soon, you'll be rocking this whole divorced, single-mom thing!

#79. Single Parents Are Superheroes

I was raised by a single mother. It wasn't easy for her or for me. I learned one thing though, my mom is a superhero. Here are some key attributes of superheroes, and if you know any single parents you will agree, they definitely fit the bill.

- Extraordinary Abilities:

  Maybe it's that they don't need sleep. Maybe they can work double shifts. Whatever their super ability, it's hard to deny these are uncommon folks.

- Fearless:

  Doing what you have to do for your kids, knowing when you need help, and holding your head up high when you feel like you're drowning takes courage.

- A Strong Moral Compass:

  Maybe being away more than other parents means you worry more about your kids' moral compass. As a result, leading by example becomes a major trait for single parents.

- Fighting Spirit and Mental Toughness:

  It's not about never falling. It's not about never crying. It's about wiping your tears and getting back up. A superhero suffers setbacks but to them, staying down is not an option.

- Knowledge:

  Superheroes are savvy, street smart, and always learning. They have seen some sh*t, and they have learned some sh*t.

  If you're a single parent, I say, "Straighten out your cape and thank you for not taking anyone's sh*t! You got this!"

FIGHTING SPIRIT AND MENTAL TOUGHNESS

FEARLESSNESS

KNOWLEDGE

EXTRAORDINARY ABILITIES

A STRONG MORAL COMPASS

SINGLE MOMS ARE SUPERHEROES

#80. Being a Multiracial Family Is a Celebration

Being a multiracial family is a celebration. A celebration of cultures. A celebration of love. A love so strong as to conquer the whispers or stares or awkward questions from strangers.

The number of multiracial Americans is growing at a rate three times faster than the population as a whole, according to the US Census Bureau. With interracial couples accounting for 15 percent of all new marriages in the US, this trend will continue. Let the celebration continue!

To dive deeper into this topic, I reached out to Erin Washington, mother of two biracial children and author of *Squats and Margaritas: A Journey to Finding Balance.* Erin shared with us her five top tips for raising a multiracial family.

1. Prepare Your Kids for Questions Before They're Asked (because they will be).

My four-year-old daughter plays so beautifully with both her white and Black cousins. She doesn't seem to notice their diversity so it was difficult for me to intentionally point out their different skin tones. But someone else will. And not having the conversation with your child can make it seem like it's almost something negative you're keeping from them. I don't want my kids to be blindsided when someone makes a comment about their skin or hair, so I will discuss it with them before they're confronted by the boy on the playground. Give your kids the tools to handle the conversation.

2. Teach Your Kids to Embrace It.

I tell my daughter that she is a beautiful little display of many different cultures. Families come in all different shades and sizes. Every person is unique and special. They're a little like their mom and a little like their dad. I tell my kids how cool it is that they get to be both white and black! "You are the perfect mix of both. You are so special and are loved to the moon and back!"

3. Let Your Kids Choose What They Identify As.

At some point, there's gonna be a box to check, and your child is going to identify with one side more than the other. Give them the framework to make their decision by exposing them to as much as you can from both sides of the family. In some cases, kids will just identify as the side of the family that they see most often. Let them experience both cultures and then decide what they identify as.

4. Find a Diverse Group of Friends (for your kids and yourself!).

Your kids will feel comfortable in such an inclusive environment, and you can learn more about your own children's heritage (even some helpful tips like how to style your biracial daughter's hair). Don't be afraid to ask!

5. Don't Get Offended By Ignorant Comments or Questions from Strangers.

These are teaching moments! Use these instances to educate your kids. When someone points out that my kids look different than me, I remind my kids that everyone is different. No two people are the same. Everyone has a different skin tone, eye color, and hair color. No one is a match! And that's what makes this world so special— no two people are alike, but we love and accept everyone, just the way they are.

Check out the books:
* *Raising Multiracial Children* by Farzana Nayani
* *Rage Against the Minivan* by Kristen Howerton
* *I'm Chocolate, You're Vanilla: Raising Healthy Black and Biracial Children in a Race-Conscious World* by Marguerite Wright

Chapter 8
TECH PROBS

This chapter explores digital babysitters, digital assistants, and other digital wonders designed to make our lives easier and also, harder. Dealing with tech probs is a defining feature of modern mom probs. So put down your phone and take a look.

#81. BOOGEYMAN DU JOUR: SCREEN TIME

It's a fact of life. Modern people require modern technology. We have smartphones, smart TVs, smart homes, and Smart cars (aren't those cute?!). Technology is so ubiquitous that I've seen babies swipe a magazine like it's an iPad and try to zoom in on a still picture. That's ok. They're babies. They'll learn.

As much as we try to unplug and digitally detox, we are forever intertwined with our handheld devices, like shiny, glass and plastic appendages. Theoretically, a chapter on screen time can be an entire standalone textbook. Hmmm…I smell a sequel!

For now, let's just focus on the realities of screen time and handling them effectively. When smartphones and tablets were first introduced, people were like, "Great! Let's get these in front of our children so they can learn to speak three languages and do algebra by age four."

Then it morphed into, "Ugh, the baby is crying again. Lemme toss him my phone." Don't worry. Shortcomings aside, screen time hasn't been all bad.

Sometimes screen time can be a bonding experience. In my house, we often sit next to each other on our respective devices and enjoy the time together. Sure, we'll occasionally say, "Honey, check out this news story," or "Mommy, play this new game I coded myself." In my case, it's, "Please read this over. Is this meme funny?" But our family mantra is, "People are always more important than screens." This is our way to say, "Look up at people when they are in front of you or are addressing you." It shows respect and that we value each other more than we do our devices.

So what's the issue? The problem arises when screen time becomes a "thing"—a thing that your child doesn't want to give up. The boogeyman is not actually screen time, but what your child may turn into if she gets too much of it. Too much screen time can lead to what I like to call the Screen Fiend, a crying, not-wanting-to-hand-over-the-device goblin. To combat the Screen Fiend, it's important to set boundaries and communicate with your children about their screen usage.

I reached out to clinical psychologist Rebecca Kennedy, PhD, for some guidance on this topic. In return, she offered the following advice.

Seven Strategies for Managing Screen Time to Help Reduce Meltdowns:

1. Clarity: We all fare better when we know what to expect. Telling your kids, "Ok, sure, you can have some iPad time… but wait, wait, not yet. Let's talk about how long and pick

an end time so we all know what to expect," is much better than, "Ok, sure, you can have some iPad time…" and then yelling upstairs to your kids at some point, "Five more minutes and then you're done!"

2. Emotional Vaccination: Before you start screen time, pause and think with your child about how ending it will feel. When we predict our tougher feelings, our body feels more in control when those feelings arrive. I also like "getting out" some of the screen-time-ending-protests with my kids with lightness and laughter; we all whine together and go through the list of complaints that tend to come up. This adds levity and connection before the difficult moment arises.

3. Wishing: Reframe your child's complaint as an unfulfilled wish and then speak to the wish your child has—often this is, "Ugh…you really wish you could have another show, huh?" or "You wish you could make screen time decisions for yourself, right?" Kids feel seen when we recognize and validate their wishes.

4. Remember Family Jobs: As parents, we have to make decisions that we think are best for our kids. Our children do not have to like these decisions. And, when our kids don't like things, it is their job to express these feelings. And it's our job to be consistent in our boundaries.

5. Shift from No to Yes: When you plan for the future, you can shift a bit to the "Yes, we can watch that show tomorrow…" instead of staying stuck in the "no" of today. Kids do well when we record their ideas and plans, as this makes things more concrete for them to hold onto.

6.   Act Out Your Own Meltdown and Recovery: Modeling our own meltdowns and then breathing and self-talk recoveries is super helpful for our kids, as they feel less alone in their big feelings and learn what realistic regulation looks like.

7.   Collaborate with Your Child: Have a family meeting in advance to discuss screen time rules. Listen to your child about how much screen time he wants, at what time of the day, what shows he wants to watch; validate your child during this meeting, saying "That's a great point" and "I hear you. Seems like that's really important to you." See if you can incorporate at least one of your child's preferences in your decisions; this will help your child have a sense of control and ownership, leading to an increased likelihood of cooperation.

The Screen Fiend doesn't need to be the monster in your house if you implement some of these tips from Dr. Kennedy. I promise you, they work, but you have to be consistent!

#82. Alexa, Take Care of These Kids: An Interview with Alexa

The interview with my son went so well that I decided to sit down with my Amazon Alexa for a nice fireside chat about parenting. Here's a transcript from our conversation:

Me: Alexa, may I ask you some questions about parenting?

Alexa: Sorry, I'm not sure.

Me: Ok…well, how do I best take care of my kids?

Alexa: Here's something I found on the web. According to square-space: exercise, meditate, take a bath.

Me: Well, how can I be a good mom?

Alexa: Try to set clear, firm rules and be consistent on the consequences. For example, if your child pushes his sibling, give him the same punishment every time. Also, you have to show good behavior and show support and show up for their games and practices. Does that answer your question?

Me: Yes.

Alexa: Great, thanks for your feedback.

Me: Alexa, how can I raise happy, good kids?

Alexa: Here's something I found from Huff Pages on the web. Offer treats and kisses to reinforce good behavior.

Me: Alexa, would you be a good mother?

Alexa: Sorry. I'm not sure.

Me: Alexa, what do I do about cranky kids?

Alexa: Leave the kids alone and let them play.

Me: Ok...well, how do I make my kids eat their dinner?

Alexa: Add salt, or whatever your kids eat it with.

Me: Pardon?

Alexa: Sorry, I don't understand.

Me: Alexa, how do I get my kids to clean their rooms?

Alexa: As soon as the kids are piled on the bus and sh*t.

Me: Huh? Ok. Alexa, final question. How do I take care of an infant?

Alexa: According to Zendesk.com you have to carry the infant on your lap.

Me: Ok, Alexa. Thanks, I think. This was…interesting.

All that technology, and Alexa's parenting style seems very 1950s. So, just to be clear, Alexa cannot help you out with this parenting gig.

#83. Video Games Are Good Now?

I grew up in the 1980s. We had an Atari, played Space Invaders, and later saw the golden age of Nintendo, Sega, and all the crazy cool stuff that came afterwards. I wouldn't consider myself a gamer by any stretch. But I remember being twelve and seeing Mortal Kombat for the first time, and all the news coverage saying it would change us into little delinquents. Or at the very least, zombies. Luckily, this didn't happen. But as a parent, I think this legacy of fear around video games has really stuck with our collective sense of where video games fit within the hierarchy of worthy pursuits.

But is it all bad? I'm not talking about clearly adult video games. And I fully acknowledge we should go outside and get exercise. I get it. I'm talking about a little Mario Kart now and then with the kiddos. So I decided to do a little research, and I have to say, it's not all bad news.

Believe it or not, most of the published studies on video games show they may benefit kids' coordination, problem-solving skills, attention, concentration, and even memory. Video games may also help improve people's vision and allow them to practice leadership skills and communication in multiplayer platforms. Of course, you should not stay in a dark room for ten days at a clip playing video games. But that's what moms are for, right? Get out of there, Honey, and grab the paper off the driveway!

Some interesting information about video games can be found by viewing the TED Talks by Daphne Bavelier, Gabe Zichermann, and Jane McGonigal. Google those names plus TED Talk and you'll see what I mean.

#84. Drowning in a Sea of Selfies: Digital Picture Overload

My 1996 self *never* could have imagined being able to take pictures on every whim. As a teenager, I took pictures with disposable wind-up cameras. Then I had to wait for two weeks to pick up the pictures from CVS (after begging my mom to drive me there). Now we take pics to remind us where we parked at Six Flags.

We take 24,567 pictures of our kids in the bath, on the sidewalk, in the food pantry, everywhere. But do we ever actually hold these pictures in our hands? Nope. Do we ever print them out? Rarely. Do we ever even look at them again? Uhhhhhh.

We have *thousands and thousands* of these silly, mundane, and sometimes adorable photos in a virtual camera roll, and they sort of disappear. Only when Facebook or Google sends you a "Memory from 2016" post do you remember how cute she was as a six-month-old. So here's some advice for putting these pictures to good use and a more strategic way of enjoying these memories.

1. Back that thang up. If you aren't storing your photos regularly on Google, SmugMug, Dropbox, or some other cloud-based service (most of which are free), you are missing out. And you are skating dangerously close to the edge of losing those precious chubby-phase photos.

2. Photobomb your kid. Moms are never in the pictures. Ever! Get in there. No one cares if you have spit-up on your shirt, your hair is dirty, or you had four hours of sleep. Your future self will thank you.

3. Don't teach your kids that photos need to be perfect. It's bad enough for your mental health to post to Instagram after a thousand shots to pretend you have no blemishes. Send the right message to your kids and to yourself; these photos are for us to document our memories, nothing more.

4. Schedule some time to review your pictures. If you keep a digital calendar, make it a quarterly practice to review all the photos, back them up, and maybe even look at some of them and enjoy.

5. Don't be *awful* by ruining every good moment as a photo op. Yes, you may be witnessing a beautiful sunset with your family. But sometimes, maybe these sunsets are best kept just for your family and experienced in the moment. Nobody watches that Fourth of July fireworks video they took, but I can say with confidence I remember the feeling of snuggling up with my husband on a picnic blanket while our son caught fireflies last Fourth of July. No photos exist of that evening, and none are needed.

#85. Your Phone: Your Greatest Lifeline and Your Greatest Distraction

You grab it. You check it. You put it down. You pick it up again. Look at the time. Put it down. Pick it up. Scroll Instagram. Lose another twenty minutes. Put it down again. Repeat every day, forever.

Admit it, you reach for your phone more often than the 1999 version of you could *ever* have imagined. Is it good? Bad? Does it matter? Common belief would lead us to believe that more phone usage in front of our children would be detrimental. And for sure, if you are ignoring your children to play Candy Crush, that's behavior you should probably work on.

However, a recent study in the Journal of Child Psychology and Psychiatry showed that, "at low levels of displacing time with family, more smartphone use was associated with better (not worse) parenting." The authors noted that especially considering diverse family environments, smartphones play multiple roles in family life, and when not heavily impacting family time, may have a positive role in parenting. *Boom!* One less thing to have mom guilt about. Again, as with everything, it's moderation. We're entitled to a little digital vacation. Don't beat yourself up.

And remember! Say it with me: People are still more important than screens.

For each pair, select the item that is more important.

Phone	Child
Phone	Significant other
Phone	Burning bag of popcorn
Phone	Stop sign
Phone	Overflowing bathtub
Phone	Flight of stairs
Phone	Busy intersection

#86. Keeping Up with the FOMO: Social Media Perfection

Social media has been good to me. I built an Instagram community by hearing the stories and jokes of mothers and by sharing my own. Social media has many positive aspects; it can be inspirational, it can forge a community, and it's good for connecting with far-away relatives or friends and for keeping up with the latest trends.

But as you likely know, social media has a darker side. It perpetuates unattainable perfection in the form of photoshopped pictures, filtered faces, and curated settings.

According to addictioncenter.com, "There is an undeniable link between social media use, negative mental health, and low self-esteem. While social media platforms have their benefits, using them too frequently can make people feel increasingly unhappy and isolated. These negative emotional reactions are not only produced due to the social pressure of sharing things with others, but also the comparison of material things and lifestyles that these sites promote."

In addition to the feelings of inadequacy you can feel from going all-in on social media, social media addiction is also a real thing. If you've ever posted content on social media and then reached for your phone to check the likes and comments again and again, you know what I mean. Anticipating all the likes and comments gives us a dopamine release, reinforcing this behavior and motivating us to do it again.

Since smartphones and social media certainly aren't going anywhere, it is up to users, like us, to modify our behavior.

As a heavy social media user, I understand the all-encompassing pressures and pings from these platforms. These are my recommendations for not getting too sucked in:

* Limit your media consumption. Use the Digital Wellbeing app on your phone or download one. You can set screen time use and screen unlock goals.

* Turn off your notifications, especially from Facebook, Instagram, TikTok, and other social platforms. Keep notifications for texting and phone calls. Your kid's school may be trying to reach you.

* Turn on Focus Mode (if your phone has the option). It will gray out and block use of your applications so you can focus for a set period of time.

* Charge your phone in a different room from your bedroom. It will reduce your temptation to grab and grab again.

* Unfollow accounts that make you feel less than or are obviously detrimental to your mental health. Don't hate-check on other accounts either. Hate-checking is scrolling through the accounts of people you secretly loathe. You're better than that. Keep it movin'!

* Remember, social media is intended to be *enjoyable*! If you find yourself not enjoying it, try to take a digital detox for a few days or a week. As hard as it may be, this will do wonders! Don't worry; there's always time to learn the latest viral dances. Here's the cheat sheet: touch your shoulders and wiggle your hips.

* If you suspect that you have or someone you love has a social media addiction, please seek professional help. www.addicitioncenter.com is a valuable resource.

THE SOCIAL MEDIA VENN

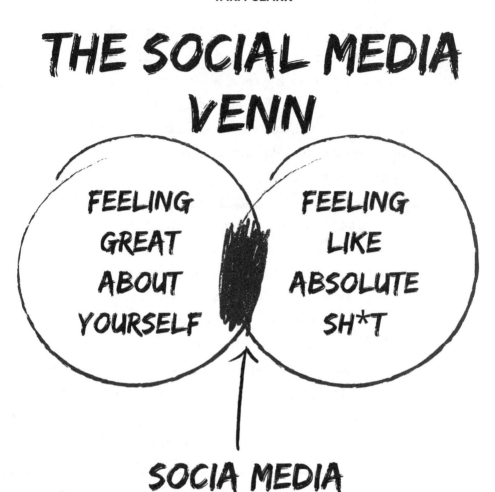

FEELING GREAT ABOUT YOURSELF

FEELING LIKE ABSOLUTE SH*T

SOCIA MEDIA

#87. FACEBOOK MOM GROUPS: YOUR SOURCE FOR DRAMA, MEMES, AND MEDICAL ADVICE

Facebook Mom Groups (FBMG) take a lot of flak because they unintentionally provide great entertainment in the form of ridiculous comments and drama. I'm part of the UES (Upper East Side) group which provides hours of "stalker-ish" fun, even though I don't live in NYC anymore. It was too good to leave. Are these women for real?

It's *Gossip Girl* meets *Sesame Street*. From $3,000 strollers to $30,000 vacations and $3,000,000 apartments they just casually list for sale, these moms have questions (and answers) for everything! It certainly is not your average mom group, but I have to admit the insanity I saw on there many years ago inspired me to launch my Instagram account! So I extend my gratitude. Thank you, ladies! Air kiss! Muah!

Crazy questions and comments aside, at the core of every FBMG is its other value—a sounding board for genuine concerns, fears, and ponderings…and memes! Laughter is crucial to making it through our harried days but so is information. With little in the way of an in-person village, modern moms find their village online. I've had questions answered about the best child-friendly barber shops and best "Mommy and Me" classes via these groups. But there are two caveats about the extent to which you should rely on the oracle of FBMG.

Doctors can be expensive, I get it. But the problem with using FBMG for medical advice is ummmmm…everything! The majority of the members of any FBMG are not licensed medical professionals able to diagnose a head contusion from your blurry camera phone picture. In fact, few actual medical professionals would do so even if they were members of the group. Be wary of accepting pediatric advice from strangers. Sure, they can recommend which baby bottles worked best for them or what toys are good for a fourth birthday. But steer clear of risking your family's health by crowd-sourcing medical advice.

Another thing to keep in mind about your local FBMG is that anyone could start one, and only recently has Facebook offered guidelines for moderation. The reason this matters is because you never really know who is on the other end of this "line," so to speak. An issue arose in the UES Moms groups regarding censorship of moms of color, which eventually led to its temporary shutdown before the introduction of new, more diverse moderators. Keep an eye out for anything off-the-wall when you join the local FBMG, and if you think you just entered a lion's den, join the FBMG for the next town over.

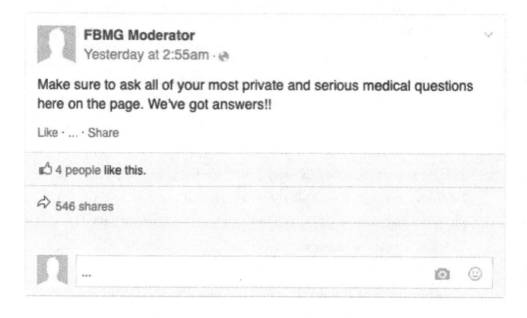

FBMG Moderator
Yesterday at 2:55am · 🌐

Make sure to ask all of your most private and serious medical questions here on the page. We've got answers!!

Like · ... · Share

👍 4 people like this.

↪ 546 shares

...

#88. I Don't Care If Billy Down the Street Has the New iPhone

Getting your child a phone is a personal choice. There are compelling reasons for and against getting your kid a phone, and those reasons change with the child's age. I cannot help you determine the "right" age for this to happen. What I can do is tell you what to do if they ask tomorrow and you aren't ready.

Here's a fun word search you can do with your kid, if they ask for a phone and you aren't quite ready.

"MAY I HAVE A PHONE?" WORD SEARCH

```
N O P E X N O C A N D O X
A B S O L U T E L Y N O T T
N A H S N E V E R L M T Y I
T R Y A G A I N D U D E Z Y
Y O G U Z I T H I N K N O T
W A I T A W H I L E Q X Z Y
W H E N U A R E O L D E R I
H A H A H A F O R G E T I T
I S O R R Y N O T S O R R Y
N O T O N Y O U R L I F E Z
```

For my international friends, here are some useful responses:

Nie, Non, No, Não, Nu, Nyet, Ne, La', M hěi, Nein, Ochi, Loh, Nahin, Ani, Méiyǒu

And finally, a big old *no freaking way*!

#89. PINTEREST IS YOUR FRENEMY

How did anyone plan anything without Pinterest? No, seriously. I'm asking you. How? I don't recall. Pinterest is like your best friend and worst enemy all rolled into one, hence frenemy status. How else would we see all of the eye-candy crafts and mouth-watering recipes floating in the world, while at the same time, feel so pressured to create this perfection in our lives? It's the go-to for party planning ideas, gender reveals, recipes, and new hair styles.

But, Modern Mom, you have to manage your expectations when going down the rabbit hole of Pins. Most of us are all familiar with Pinterest fails. You see a beautiful 3D kitten-shaped birthday cake. You try to make said cake, and it turns out looking like a pile of kitten poop.

Pinterest is a platform that should be used as a resource for ideas and not a mirror to reflect or reinforce our imperfections. Just because your nursery looks like a raccoon lives in it doesn't mean you're a messy person. Just because you can't decorate a three-tier fondant cake in the shape of Olaf doesn't make you an inadequate person. Strong effort, though!

#90. WHAT'S A COMMERCIAL, MOMMY? THE ON-DEMAND CHILD

Let's face it. Your kid is an on-demand kid. From the repeated *Paw Patrol* episodes to those near meltdowns when they think they missed their favorite part of that Disney movie and you just start it up again. We've come a long way since Saturday morning cartoons. Let's consider how things have changed, what we've gained, and what we've lost.

Modern kids will scarcely know the feeling of waiting around for the premiere of the new *Thundercats* episode or knowing that *Duck Tales* is about to start.

But…

They will also never have to get up from their couch to change the channel or watch cartoons on a tiny ten-inch box with a grainy picture and horrible sound.

Modern kids will never know the excitement of seeing the newest Holiday Barbie commercial and running to get their mom so they can say, "Tell Santa I want *that!*"

But…

They will also never have to spend ten minutes of every half hour being marketed to while watching their shows. They will also never have to slip and break their wrist because they heard that Barbie commercial from the other room, and they ran to see it before it disappeared.

Modern kids will never know the fun of appointment viewing for special events like the yearly *Wizard of Oz* showing, the *Magical World of Disney*, or *Cosmos.*

But…

They will never know what life was like before being able to snuggle up with you whenever it's convenient and have a family movie night or even a double feature of Frozen I and II.

So I say, embrace the on-demand world, grab some snacks, and use its power for good!

#91. DON'T BE A TROLL: DIGITAL CITIZENSHIP EXPLAINED

You interact with technology every day, but do you know what it means to be a good digital citizen? I didn't think so. As your tour guide, I'm here to help. In the book *Digital Citizenship in Schools*, authors Mike Ribble and Gerald Bailey explain the nine elements of digital citizenship.

As a modern mom, you should read these elements, and I conveniently broke them down into real talk.

* Digital Access: full electronic participation in society. Give everyone access to computers and internet.
* Digital Commerce: electronic buying and selling of goods and services. Don't rip people off.
* Digital Communication: electronic exchange of information. Be honest in your words.
* Digital Literacy: teaching and learning about technology and its use. Learn some sh*t.
* Digital Etiquette: electronic standards of conduct or procedure. Don't be a jerk.
* Digital Law: electronic responsibility for actions and deeds. Don't steal sh*t that isn't yours.
* Digital Rights and Responsibilities: those freedoms extended to everyone in the digital world. Be respectful.

* Digital Health and Wellness: physical and psychological well-being in the digital world. Don't spend all of your time online.
* Digital Security: electronic precautions to guarantee safety. Don't hack sh*t.

The more you know....

Literally Everybody
@errbody

Don't hack sh*t. Don't steal sh*t. Don't be a jerk.

12:00 PM · Jun 1, 2020

32 Retweets   **348** Likes

#92. INFORMATION OVERLOAD: THANKS A LOT, GOOGLE

Dr. Google is open at 3:00 AM. Dr. Google doesn't have co-pays. Dr. Google knows all.

Dr. Google isn't a doctor.

The internet is a tool intended to help us, not overwhelm us. Google is at the center of most of what we do on the internet.

Most new modern moms have searched Google to answer all of life's mysteries about their little cherubs.

Is this much spit-up normal?

Why does his poop look like that?

Based on the search, the user may receive the correct information, or she may go down a rabbit hole of doom-scrolling, frantically checking the next article or the next website. One article leads to the next to the next to the next. Sometimes, a partial search yields suggestions that suck the user in. Thirty minutes later, the reader is still sitting on the toilet learning about the efficiency of bamboo diapers. We've all been there. Maybe not necessarily on the toilet but scrolling *ad infinitum.*

With too much information, our thoughts can start to spin, sometimes out of control. To prevent that, we need to ask ourselves questions, popular in Cognitive Behavioral Therapy.

1.) How are my thoughts behaving?

2.) Are they useful?

3.) What can I do about them?

Are our thoughts making us behave in a way other than how we would act if we didn't have all of this information? The 24/7 news cycle, love it or hate it, leads to anxiety. Continuously hearing about COVID, the economy, and the state of the world is exhausting on our psyches. Add to that our scrolling for more information about the safest baby products, best parenting practices, handling meal prep, and the cutest summer shoes; it's too much to handle in a sane way. Overload leads to confusion, anxiety, and decision paralysis.

Here are my recommendations for when information overload creeps in like a pop-up ad in your brain:

1. Clear your mind. If you find yourself down a rabbit hole, take a deep breath and ask yourself, "What am I looking to get out of this?"

2. Be deliberate in your media consumption, even on social media. Unfollow accounts that don't spark joy. Don't keep the twenty-four-hour news on for twenty-four hours a day.

3. Keep it simple. If you are researching a new baby product, limit it to no more than three choices and research those thoroughly. No need to overwhelm yourself with extraneous things all to have no decision made by the end of your scrolling.

4. Remember that your computer is not your doctor. If you have real medical concerns, don't stay up until 2:00 AM searching for the medical answers on WebMD. Reach out to a medical professional in real life or call 911 in an emergency.

To illustrate how tricky Google searches can be, these are the suggestions for some open-ended parenting searches.

Is my kid...

-on the spectrum

-color blind

-depressed

-hurting

-ready to potty train

Is my child...

-autistic

-ready for kindergarten

-gifted

-bipolar

-overweight

-on the spectrum

Is my daughter…
    -autistic

    -bipolar

    -a narcissist

    -depressed

Is my baby…
    -teething

    -colic

    -autistic

    -sick

    -eating enough

    -too big

    -sleeping enough

Why does my kid…
    -hate writing

    -have a fever

    -hate me

    -have no friends

    -ney bean recipe have no flavor

How can I get my child to…
    -lose weight

    -gain weight

    -eat

    -poop

    -sleep

    -stop biting his nails

    -stop vaping

Based on those searches, it's obvious that information overload can lead parents' thoughts to spiral out of control with, "What's wrong with my kid?" "Why does everything seem to be wrong all the time?" "Why am I failing as a parent?" It's the modern version of Mean World Syndrome, a phenomenon developed by the incredibly brilliant media scholar George Gerbner (who happened to be a college professor of mine).

"Mean world syndrome is a cognitive bias where people perceive the world to be more dangerous than it actually is due to long-term, moderate to heavy exposure to violence-related content on mass media."

Simply put, the more we scroll the internet, the worse off we think our children are in this big mean world. Without turning this into a college term paper, which I would gladly write again for the late Dr. Gerbner, this piece of information is important for your well-being.

For the health of you and your family, limit your information and media consumption in our 24/7/365 information-spewing world. Stay informed, by all means. But remember, kids are kids who are going to do what kids do. And the world is a big place where crazy stuff sometimes happens. Don't drive yourself bonkers non-stop with the particulars.

Now if we could just get our kidney beans to have flavor...look at the search results again if you missed that gem.

#93. Distance Learning: Zoom Me Right Outta Here

FAAAACCCCCKKKKKKKKK

Now that I have that out of my system, *phew*! I feel better.

As if modern life wasn't complicated enough, throw a global pandemic into the mix. With it came the need to educate our school-aged children outside of the physical classroom. If you were a mom not homeschooling her kids, welp, those days are gone.

Enter distance learning.

Distance learning is education outside of the classroom via virtual meetings and independent assignments. It's a new phenomenon for many parents and especially challenging for parents who work outside the home and for those who work outside the home *in* the home. The key to adjusting to our new reality is knowing when to walk away from a taxing situation.

I'm too new at this to do anything but send good vibes. Good luck! Hang in there! Hopefully this isn't forever. In the meantime, don't throw your children or your computer out the window! One bit of advice we just figured out: use headphones for virtual classroom sessions. If your kid is tethered to the computer with kid-friendly headphones it seems to go better; it filters out all the distractions and sends the message, you need to sit here and pay attention now.

I'll leave you with a fun little word jumble for you to play while your kids sit through another Zoom class:

SI SHTI ARPC EVOR EYT ?

> *Answer:*
> *Is this crap over yet?*

WHEN YOUR SINGLE FRIENDS TOOK AN EXOTIC VACATION AND YOU'RE PROUD YOU TOOK A SHOWER.

Chapter 9
TRAVEL PROBS

Sounds glamorous, no? Also, it seems random to include a chapter on travel, of all things. Well, let me tell you, going anywhere with kids counts as travel. Sorry. Going to Grandma's house? Travel. Packing up for a day at the beach? Travel. Leaving the house for a trip that requires you to get out of your pajamas? Travel. This group of miscellaneous problems transcend just one topic but need to have a spotlight shined on them.

#94. PERILOUS PLACES

You go lots of places with your kids. And they can't all be glamorous. Here's a rapid-fire, high-yield list of some perilous places and the things you need to know to get out of each unscathed.

* Gift shops: My most dreaded realization at any aquarium or museum is that we need to exit through the gift shop. The only thing that works for us is we just say, "It was very expensive to get in here and we're out of money." Move quickly! Kids cannot resist a rubber dinosaur or plush octopus.

* Trampoline parks: Sign life away. Put on special socks that protect you from nothing. Pray that their bones are strong, and that's all you can do.

* Water parks: Great fun. We love 'em. Watch out for idiot adults if your child is a lingerer at the bottom of slides. Also, a swim diaper for the little ones. Don't be the family who shuts down the whole thing, please.

* Ball pits and foam pits: Spit-covered plastic balls? Uh, no thanks. Spongy pit of bacteria? We're good. If you have to choose one, I say foam pit because at least it's soft. Hey ball pit, 1986 called and it wants its suffocation pit back.

* Zoos: Hot and smelly. But the popcorn and lemonade is always delish. Bring or rent a freakin' stroller and enjoy the animals. Kids usually don't last too long and then you can finish that salty, buttery treat. But beware! See above about gift shops.

* County fairs and carnivals: Americana at its finest. Introduce your kid to cotton candy. Stay up late. Avoid the dart attraction with the balloons. I once saw a dart bounce back and hit a kid right below the eye. Play the squirt gun thing as a family, corner the market on a cheaply-made stuffy, and call it a night before you drop Vegas-level cash.

* Grandma's house: From the time they get there to the time they leave, they will be eating candy and pure processed garbage. You will get whatever break or time you need out of the deal, but you will not be picking up your child the next morning, only a beast that physically resembles your child. Rest up!

* Malls/toy stores: Do not. And I repeat. Do not purchase a birthday gift for one of your kid's classmates while your kid is with you. This should be obvious, but I'm just putting it out there. If you absolutely must bring her to the store, have a heart-to-heart conversation with your child about sharing and giving.

* Target/Walmart: See my method for getting through the gift shop and employ as needed.

Things to say in order to get out of the gift shop with wallet intact:
* *Nah, we're good.*
* *No, thank you.*
* *Hey, is that (insert favorite character, superhero, princess here)?*
* *Nope.*
* *We have one just like that at home. Remember?*
* *Nuh-uh.*

#95. FAMILY VACATIONS (SHOULD INCLUDE AT LEAST TWO RECOVERY DAYS AFTER THEY'RE DONE)

I hate to beat a dead horse, but…lower those expectations, Mama, you're going on vacation. There are few hard and fast rules for every family that will get you there and back in one piece, but here's the best I could come up with to determine whether you will have fun on vacation:

Ok, so maybe your trip will be fun, but you're gonna be exhausted, Mama. Pack as many toys and books from home as you can and take a look at some air travel advice below.

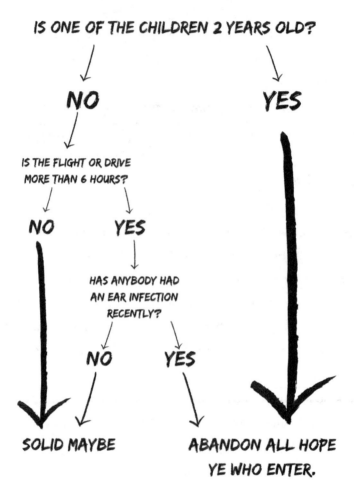

WILL THIS VACAY BE ENJOYABLE?

IS ONE OF THE CHILDREN 2 YEARS OLD?

NO — YES

IS THE FLIGHT OR DRIVE MORE THAN 6 HOURS?

NO — YES

HAS ANYBODY HAD AN EAR INFECTION RECENTLY?

NO — YES

SOLID MAYBE — ABANDON ALL HOPE YE WHO ENTER.

#96. AIR TRAVEL, A TIMELINE

Have you ever run a marathon? Ever fled from a natural disaster? Maybe not, but you will absolutely learn what that bodily sensation is like through the wonders and glamour of air travel. From the moment you wake up until you arrive at your destination, your hairs will start graying, and your heart will be racing. The true magic of air travel lies in the age of your youngins, so here's a rough timeline of how that's gonna go.

- 0–3 months old. Congratulations! You and your baby burrito can go wherever your pediatrician says you are allowed to go. Keep that baby fed and change that diaper in the cramped bathroom, and you're gonna think, "We got this! We're going places."

- 3–9 months old. Ok, I hope you brought enough formula and/or your breasts are ready. Bring a favorite toy, but for the most part your job now is timing those feedings with takeoff and landing so those little ears are protected. Watch out for the ignorant, unfeeling, horrible adults around you who don't understand that kids cry, but kids also have to go places sometimes because you can't leave them at home for three days. Anyways, have your husband pop in your ear buds and just cruise. Oh, remember to keep an eye on that formula once it's mixed in a bottle. We once had a whole bottle explode in the overhead bin and leak all over the people behind us. They were nice about it, but it was pretty mortifying and the baby formula smells god-awful. You got this!?!?

- 9–36 months old. You don't got this. Really, you should stay the F home. What's wrong with you? You knew better, and you decided to go anyway. From mopping the floor in the terminal with their mouths, to screaming uncontrollably on the plane, this is the true test of the traveling family. I am offering zero advice here besides, I told you so. You couldn't drive. You *had* to fly....

- 3–5 years old. Ok, keep it short and sweet. Tablets, flashcards, coloring books, storybooks, toys, and constant changes between these. Tell them the button that reclines the chairs makes the plane take off and land. Come up with something, but you may be able to pull this one off now.
- 5–10 years old. You good, Mama. Just don't push too hard. Little legs, little eardrums, little attention span. Just don't let your guard down and at least the payoff will be a piña colada somewhere tropical while you try to keep them from getting buried in sand.

PARENT SWEAT METER

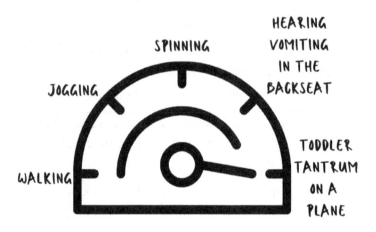

#97. CAR TRIPS

"Are we there yet?" Good question, kiddo. Other questions to add to this line of inquiry include:

"Why did we do this?"

"When is the next rest stop?"

"What made me think we could get by without a tablet?"

"How am I going to reach that stray toy that fell under my seat to prevent the next meltdown?"

"When will I learn?"

If you have answers to these questions, then go ahead, take a six-hour road trip. If not, you better look in the mirror, get some Rocky montage music going, and prepare for the long goodbye to sanity via the great American highway. Here's a sample itinerary for you as you go to that destination with the fam.

* The departure: Plan to get going bright and early because you want to squeeze the most out of the day. Just know your kids may have other plans.

* Car sickness: This may not apply to all of you, but if you have a kid prone to car sickness, please understand that they will get sick no sooner than thirty minutes but no later than ninety minutes into the trip. That's just long enough to be past the point of no return but too short to make that vomit smell tolerable for just a bit longer. Hope you enjoy the next four to five hours of sour milk smell, because it's going to be your air freshener du jour. Hopefully you're headed to a water park and can drown it out with the chlorine smell.

* Boredom: This will set in in about the same time frame. Sure, you packed the books, the tablets, the games. Hey, you even planned a few eye-spy distractions. But I'm sorry, Mama, this is boring. Are we there yet?

* Food: I don't want Cheerios, I'm hungry for real food. Ok, we can stop and get you a Happy Meal with a toy. Oh, you're

so distracted by the new toy that your food got cold and now you don't want it anymore. Typical....

* Conflict resolution: "Mom! She won't stop staring at me! I was not! He's breathing on me!" Ok, Mama, you got this. Backseat quarreling was just as inevitable as early-onset boredom. Erect some tall cardboard dividers between their seats. Enjoy the peace. You're welcome.

* Rest stops: You can't drink alcohol, so you've been nervously sipping that iced coffee you got a few clicks back, and now you have to pee. Do they have to pee as well, or can you just go? They're fine. Until you hit the road again. When you get out to pee, they *have to* get out and pee as well. No excuses. No questions asked. Make them pee.

* Meltdowns: You will all have a meltdown of some sort. You may all threaten to "turn this car around" at some point. Embrace the meltdown and drown it out with some soothing music as necessary. If you have a significant other, make a pact not to fight and to join forces against the hooligans in the back seat.

* More boredom: I guess this was inevitable too, huh? You really had to take a six-hour road trip?

* The arrival: Get ready for it..."Mom, can we go back home?" (Looks into the camera The Office-style.)

#98. How F*cked Is My Car Now?

My first car was my mom's ten-year-old Nissan. It wasn't much, but it was mine. I had a lot of great memories in that car. Road trips with the windows down and the radio blasting. Commutes to my summer jobs. Packing it up to go to college. I have always had a fondness in my heart for my car. In a way, a car is a second home.

These days, my car is by all objective standards a nicer, quieter, newer vehicle than that old Nissan. And yet…it is completely F'd. Yours is about to be, too, if it isn't already. My advice is only enough to keep your car *functional*. It will never be that vehicle of freedom and fun that it was in the past. But it's the best you got. Here are some pointers (slaps the hood).

* Lease versus buy? Ah, the age-old question among car shoppers. Sure, you can go on YouTube and learn all about the risks and benefits of both options, but here's the truth: *Buy* the car if you are ok staring at that gash in the backseat for ten years. The foam that pours out will make a nice stress toy on long trips. *Lease* the car if you enjoy doing magic, because when it comes time to turn the car in you will have to make lots of imperfections disappear or prepare to be taken to the cleaners. It's really a wash, so do whatever you want.

* Dark interior scuffs. Light interior gets dirty. Having had both, it's black interior for me, every time. But really, 1970s brown is probably the ideal color for the most amount of camouflage, and you can't do that; you have to have some standards. Right?

* Target bags times ten for garbage, garbage, garbage.

* No chocolate. Ever. Don't kid yourself.

* No unsupervised gum until age seven. If they sit behind you, it's in your hair or their hair, and no place in between. Well, maybe in between the seats where it will melt and be stuck on forever.

* Blanket for impromptu picnics, spills, or for cold little legs.

* Treasures such as rocks, pine cones, sticks, bricks, and dead spiders go in the trunk. They're coming home with you, so just have that blanket back there to lay that stuff down on until you get home. Throw them out a day or two later when the kiddos forget about them.
* Baby wipes no matter what age they are.
* A first aid kit, of course.
* Bottled water—because you never know.
* Diapers (even a few years after potty-training). Trust me.
* Always, always, always carry an extra set of clothes.

Your car is now F'd, but at least it's filled with loads of useful stuff.

CAR (PRE-KIDS)

CAR (WITH KIDS)

#99. The Beach (Has a Lot of Sand on It)

There are few greater joys than a day at the beach. The smell of the salty air. The sun. The sound of the waves. Your toes in the sand. The sand in your two-year old's mouth, and now his ears, and now his eyes. Ahhhhhh!! What were we thinking?

If you're like me, you think lying out at the beach is the ideal way to spend your day. Stop it. Adjust now to using the lens of the slowly-aging parent and you will see the beach for what it is, a minefield of epic proportions. Several perils await, as outlined below:

* The Sun: This evil ball of magic will seek out those missed spots of skin where your child's SPF 1000, T-shirt-in-a-can, non-hypoallergenic, uber-pricey sunscreen could not cover. And you will pay for it with a one-inch strip of sunburn that will bubble up and remind you that you are not fit to be a parent. Buy five gallons of the best SPF you can afford, pour it in a bucket from Home Depot, and dip the child every thirty minutes to avoid such peril.

* The Ocean: Nothing says, "Feed me your baby," like this massive sea-monster, just laughing at you every ten seconds with each crash of the wave. And make no mistake, that sound is a lullaby that will draw in your unsteady toddler so that she runs headlong into the abyss as soon as you turn to open up that can of sunscreen for your own shoulders. Mission One at the beach is distracting the child from the whole reason you came to the beach in the first place, so you can at least get your own sh*t sorted out and have time to limber up for the wind sprints you will be doing every time she heads for certain peril.

* The Sand: Screw you, sand! Is your child interested in putting things in his mouth? Perfect, here are a trillion pieces of sand for him to enjoy. Not interested? Doesn't matter. He's got his hands coated in sand now, and those hands are going into his mouth at some point, and so, too, will go the sand. And that's if you're lucky, maybe he has to rub his eyes. Oh, not an eye rubber? That's ok, there's wind. Another invisible force just transporting these microscopic eye-daggers your way and converging in one place: your child's eyeballs. Be sure to pack extra water, not only to stay hydrated but to also use as eye-wash when the sand inevitably gets in their eyes. Hey, maybe you can get your kid to wear sunglasses. We never could, but good luck to you!

Overall, you better really like the beach. It's gonna be a perfect storm. Get a big-ass umbrella, bring lots of snacks, and get a king size blanket to lay on so there's less chance of falling into the eye-dagger sand.

Mama,

Remember when you found out you were pregnant and thought "How am I going to do this?" You did.

Remember when you had a crying newborn and thought "How am I going to get through this?" You did.

Remember when you had a strong-willed, defiant toddler and thought "How am I going to make it through?" You did.

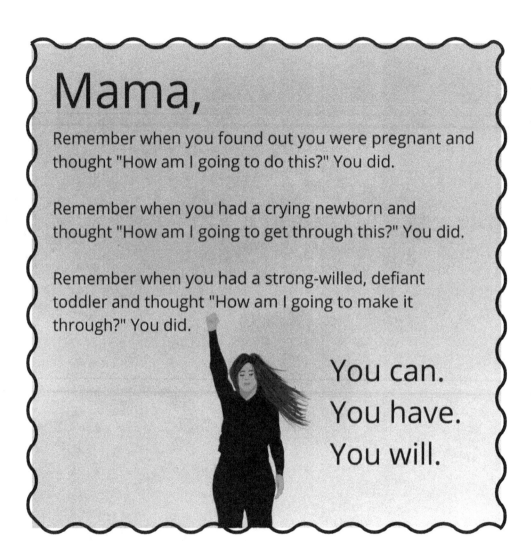

You can.
You have.
You will.

Chapter 10

I GOT 99 PROBLEMS, BUT MOTHERHOOD AIN'T ONE

Well, that concludes our tour of modern mom probs!

We laughed, we cried, we nicknamed a baby Wrinkles McWrinkleface.

It's difficult and unnecessary to say whether we modern moms have it better or worse than mothers of the past. And maybe that realization is exactly what defines us. We're the generation that not only leaned in, but we also locked down and stepped up. We don't have to compare ourselves to any prior group of moms or any societal expectations of how we should raise our kids. We have to show up for our kids, raise them to be kind, and manage our expectations of them and of ourselves.

So here's my closing advice:

* Keep laughing. Kids are adorable, hilarious, and the true joy of life.

* Keep trying. They're impossible to figure out and do crazy stuff, but they rely on us to be available so they can make sense of this world. Stay in it!

* Manage your expectations. This is the only way to keep from feeling like a constant failure. You are not a failure.

* Find time for yourself, but don't expect it to feel "balanced." Strive for "effectiveness." You're busy and overwhelmed sometimes, I know. Do what you can to find meaning in your motherhood and acknowledge that won't always mean you're happy and well-rested.

* Ask for help. If it gets to be too much, the only way out is to get help. Whether that means a mental health provider, dropping the kids off with their friends, or telling your husband it's his turn to manage the 3:00 AM feeding. Asking for help does not equate with failing!

* Support each other. Although every mom leads a different life, there is no reason to tear people down. You may not agree with all of other mom's decisions but as long as she's not harming herself or others, it doesn't give anyone the right to shame her. Celebrate the similarities and differences in our motherhood journey.

Modern moms may have 99 problems, but motherhood ain't one. We are intelligent, empowered, inclusive, courageous women who embrace this modern world despite the challenges life throws at us. We show up and we thrive. We pass it on to our children.

Because we can, we have, and we will.

Final Exam

True/ False

(Graded on a Pass/Fail System)

1.) Car naps after 4:00 PM do not destroy bedtime.
True   False

2.) Fast food tastes better when kids are strapped in their car seats.
True   False

3.) It's perfectly fine to judge a mom on her phone at the playground because you know exactly what is going on in her life.
True   False

4.) Social media is an accurate yardstick by
which to measure your own happiness.
True   False

5.) Effectiveness is more important than balance as a mother.
True   False

6.) Babies come with a universal operating manual like a Honda Pilot.
True   False

7.) Yoga pants are only to be used for yoga.
True   False

8.) It is unacceptable to wrap a birthday present in the parking lot of the birthday party venue.
True   False

9.) Flipping over chicken nuggets in the oven is synonymous with a mother's love.
True   False

10.) Including new moms in the friend group is a core tenet of the mom code.
True   False

Extra Credit:
Modern moms are intelligent, empowered, inclusive, courageous women who embrace this modern world despite the challenges life throws at us.
True   False

Answer Key:
1.) False
2.) True
3.) False
4.) False
5.) True
6.) False
7.) False
8.) False
9.) False
10.) True

Extra Credit:

True

Congratulations! You passed with flying colors! You are a bona fide Modern Mom! Now you can celebrate by posting about it.

Acknowledgments

To my loving husband, Sam. I could not have done this without you. And literally, any of this. Become a mother. Start a parenting account. Write a book. Without you, none of this would ever have happened. Thank you from the bottom of my heart. You are everything.

To Jack, my inspiration, my greatest joy, and favorite cuddle buddy. Thank you for being patient with me as I wrote this book while we were home during quarantine. I'll always remember sitting next to you at the kitchen island as you coded and I typed. Thank you for always being by my side.

To Mary, my creative illustrator, who is always ready with a cup of coffee and a laugh. I cherish our creative sessions together in the kitchen (yours *and* mine) and I cherish our friendship. I should probably be thanking the Jura coffee machine in this section, too.

To Angela, my Insta bestie. Thank you from the bottom of my heart for reviewing these chapters and always supporting me for all of these years. Someday we'll actually get to meet, and I'm going to give you the biggest hug *ever*!

To Krista, my go-to for everything! No one is on my speed-dial (or WhatsApp chat) faster than you are. You are the first person I bounce an idea off of and the best person to go to a cowboy ghost town with.

To all of the experts who graciously contributed their knowledge and skill set to this book: THANK YOU! I am eternally grateful.

To Joelle, my fearless agent, who took on a new client at the onset of the pandemic. Without you, this project would not have taken flight. Thank you for your wisdom and guidance throughout this entire process.

Photo by Mary McConville

Illustrations by Mary McConville

About the Author

*T*his is Tara's first time as a tour guide unless she's giving guests a tour of her house (which she is adept at rage-cleaning). She is the creator of the popular Instagram account @modernmomprobs. She lives in New Jersey with her husband, son, two cats, a fish, one zillion Pokémon cards, and a partridge in a pear tree.